Confused by Grace

Phill Sacre

Table of Contents

Introduction

Confused by grace?

Grace is at the heart of Christianity. Grace means that God accepts us as we are, sinners. We don't have to earn it; it is simply free and complete forgiveness through the blood of Jesus Christ. In the words of Billy Graham's favourite hymn, *Just as I am*:

> Just as I am, without one plea,
> but that thy blood was shed for me,
> and that thou bid'st me come to thee,
> O Lamb of God, I come.

What a wonderful teaching – we can come to Jesus just as we are, and he forgives us and accepts us. We can't earn our salvation, the only thing we can plead before God is the blood of Jesus Christ. One man in our church said that when he came to Christ, it was like a burden had been lifted from him. He came to Christ burdened by sin, and Christ forgave him and released him. Hallelujah!

But, once our sins are forgiven, the question arises: *what next?* We know that our lives should change, and we should come to obey God. But we also know that our obedience doesn't contribute to our salvation. Or does it? Maybe in your Bible reading, you come across passages like this from Deuteronomy 28:

> All these blessings will come on you and accompany you if you
> obey the Lord your God... (v2)

> However, if you do not obey the Lord your God and do not
> carefully follow all his commands and decrees I am giving you
> today, all these curses will come on you and overtake you. (v15)

In these verses, Moses tells the Israelites that God would punish or
reward them depending on their obedience to him. Does that mean their
salvation depended on their obedience after all? You can find lots of
places in the Old Testament prophets where God judges his people
because of their sin.

Some people say that's just the Old Testament, and things are different
now for Christians. But this is not true, you can find many similar
passages in the New Testament:

> Be perfect, therefore, as your heavenly Father is perfect.
> *Matthew 5:48*

> If we deliberately keep on sinning after we have received the
> knowledge of the truth, no sacrifice for sins is left, but only a
> fearful expectation of judgment and of raging fire that will
> consume the enemies of God. *Hebrews 10:26-27*

> Do not be deceived: Neither the sexually immoral nor idolaters
> nor adulterers nor men who have sex with men nor thieves nor
> the greedy nor drunkards nor slanderers nor swindlers will
> inherit the kingdom of God. *1 Corinthians 6:9-10*

> No one who lives in him keeps on sinning. No one who continues
> to sin has either seen him or known him. *1 John 3:6*

So, how do you square that circle?

- Does grace mean that we still must obey God?
- But then, won't God just forgive us for the times when we fail?
- But then again, how do we know that we've tried hard enough?

Is it any wonder that many people are confused by grace?! If you can identify with this confusion, then read on – this book is for you!

Cheap grace

The root of the problem is that we don't think deeply enough about the relationship between grace and the Christian life.

Many Christians have, like me, been brought up with the gospel message: "Jesus died on the cross to forgive our sins". We know that we are not saved through our own merit or efforts – we are saved *only* by grace. The apostle Paul says: "For it is by grace you have been saved, through faith... not by works, so that no one can boast" (Ephesians 2:8-9). We are saved by grace alone, and categorically not through our own good works. When I was confirmed, the bishop quoted Jonathan Edwards in his sermon: "we contribute nothing to our own salvation except the sin that made it necessary". Perhaps that's a familiar quotation to you as well.

But grace without making a difference in our lives is not grace at all. Dietrich Bonhoeffer realised that grace without a changed life was meaningless – it was what he called "cheap grace":

> Cheap grace is the preaching of forgiveness without requiring repentance, baptism without church discipline, Communion without confession, absolution without personal confession.

7

> Cheap grace is grace without discipleship, grace without the
> cross, grace without Jesus Christ, living and incarnate.[1]

Clearly, grace does not mean that we can go on to live as we like! Paul says that grace "teaches us to say 'No' to ungodliness and worldly passions, and to live self-controlled, upright and godly lives" (Titus 2:12). Grace is our teacher in how to live rightly. But how? **How does grace connect to obedience?**

If you've ever struggled with these questions, then fear not – you are not alone! I have struggled with them too. This book is an attempt to set down in words what I have learned as I have wrestled with God and the Scriptures. I have made many mistakes along the way and gone down many wrong paths – but the Lord has used them to lead me to a better understanding of the relationship between grace and obedience.

Let me tell you a little of the journey I've been on which let me to writing this book.

Walking the tightrope

One of the biggest mistakes that I made was thinking for many years that the Christian life was a kind of tightrope. You *try* to obey God (i.e., keep the Ten Commandments), but God's forgiveness (i.e., grace) is there when you fail.

It was a kind of compromise: I ended up thinking the Christian life was a balancing act, with obedience to the law on one hand and grace on the other. Christians were trying to walk a tightrope, making sure that 'grace' and 'law' were in proportion to one another.

---

[1] Dietrich Bonhoeffer, *The Cost of Discipleship* (Touchstone: 1995), 44-5

Perhaps this understanding of the Christian life is recognisable to you, too. I believe it is a common one.

The problem with this view is that it led to constant feelings of guilt. I felt guilty that I wasn't trying hard enough; guilty that I wasn't living enough for God; and guilty that I wasn't doing well enough at conquering sin. Try as I might, I couldn't stop *wanting* the wrong things. I kept praying that God would help me to stop doing the wrong things – but little seemed to help, and nothing much changed in my life.

I often ended up feeling that I was abusing God's grace – whenever I went back to a sinful pattern of behaviour, coming back to God for forgiveness *again* seemed like a burden! From conversations I have had since then, I think this is a very common experience.

9

Terrified of temptation

There was one issue which helped me more than anything to clarify my thinking about grace and obedience. That issue was friendship with the opposite sex.

I have always been a man who finds it easier to relate to women than my fellow men. Even as far back as primary school, I remember being friends with a girl in my class and my classmates making fun of me for it. However, like every normal teenager, as I grew I started to become aware of the sexual dimension of life and the complications this can introduce into relationships.

At the same time, from a young age I was taught the importance of living by the Ten Commandments. The commandment which always gave me most anxiety was "Thou Shalt Not Commit Adultery". As a young man, it seemed very contrary to my natural inclinations – not to mention the fact that we live in a world which is saturated with sexual imagery and pornography. It's a very difficult world to live in if you struggle with sexual temptation.

While I was at theological college, I became more and more anxious about keeping this command. There were so many things that fed my anxiety: we were told about the many temptations there were as pastors. We heard stories of pastors who had lost their ministries due to falling into temptation. We had books such as *Dangerous Calling* [2] recommended to us, which contained various accounts of how pastors had fallen into temptation (with disastrous consequences). We took safeguarding training, which included terrible accounts of the damage pastors had done when they had fallen into sexual sin. We studied Bible

---

[2] Paul Tripp, *Dangerous Calling* (Crossway: 2012)

verses such as Hebrews 13:4, "Marriage should be honoured by all, and the marriage bed kept pure, for God will judge the adulterer and all the sexually immoral." It was enough to make anyone terrified of what might happen!

I was determined not to be another statistic and fall into temptation. At the same time, I was very aware that I was not strong enough in myself to keep this command. My mind was filled with visions of what temptations lay in pastoral ministry, and how easily it could happen to me. I pleaded with God many times to prevent me from falling into sin. I remember praying during our daily college chapel services for God to keep me pure.

When the penny dropped

Fast forward a year or two. I finished college and my wife and nine-month-old daughter moved to a new town as I started my curacy.[3] Due to having a baby at the time, I started helping with our church baby & toddler group. One thing you can say about toddler groups is – there are always plenty of women! I was one of the few dads who attended.

Think about it for a moment: for a man struggling with sexual temptation, could there be anything worse than being surrounded by lots of young women? And yet, this was the moment that God used to bring me to a fresh understanding of his ways.

---

[3] A curacy is a bit like an apprenticeship in the Church of England for those who have finished theological college and are on their way to becoming vicars. It's the practical side of training – being in a church and learning the nuts and bolts of what it means to be a vicar. They usually last for three or four years.

As I started to build relationships with the mums at the group, it became clear to me that I had a choice:

- Keep them at arm's length out of fear of temptation.
- Move towards them in love, in the faith that God would help me do the right thing.

During those early months, God helped me to see that the path he wanted me to take was *love*. He led me to understand that I could trust him to handle temptation, and give me the love I needed to do what was right. I began to see that God wanted us to act, not from *fear* of breaking the law, but out of *love* for others. Over time, I came to see that fear and love are opposites – and God desires love, not fear.

The reason I was so terrified of breaking God's law to start with is because I knew the power of temptation. I could feel it in my own life, but I had also seen many examples through history of people who had given in to temptation with disastrous consequences. To put it bluntly, it seemed like there was a lot to fear! But it turns out that God does not want us to dwell on those fears.

Putting the pieces together

Over the last few years, I have thought more deeply about the law and its relationship to grace. In my exploration, I have found that the Bible and my experience both point in one direction. The way that I used to understand the Christian life – the tightrope walk between law and grace – was wrong.

The Christian life is not law and fear, or some kind of mixture of grace and law. God's way is *love*, pure and simple – and love itself is the fulfilment of the law. In this book, I am going to work through the Bible with you to help you understand what I've come to see. By the end of this book, I hope that you will have a deeper understanding of how the Christian life works, and how God calls us to live a life of love and not fear. My aim is that this will be more than an intellectual exercise but will teach you how to put this into practice in your life right away.

Chapter One: The purpose of the Law

Which law?

The first thing to clear up when we talk about "the law" is, which law exactly are we talking about? Sometimes in the Bible this is a reference to the first five books of the Bible (known as the Pentateuch). Sometimes it refers to *all* the Jewish ceremonial law – such as circumcision, the system of sacrifices, and so on.

The New Testament makes clear that some laws have been abrogated for Christians. For example, Mark's gospel adds the comment that Jesus declared all foods clean (Mark 7:19). This means that Christians do not have to obey the food purity laws of the Pentateuch. The million-dollar question for us, therefore, is *which* laws are still in force today and which can we ignore?

Christians have often been accused of inconsistency in which Old Testament laws they choose to apply. For example, there's a scene in *The West Wing* where the President talks to a doctor who calls homosexuality an 'abomination' on her radio show. As she points out, "The Bible calls homosexuality an abomination – Leviticus 18:22". The President then questions her about other laws from Leviticus – for example, what price he should ask for his daughter when he sells her into slavery (as permitted in the law). The implication is, she is a hypocrite for cherry-picking the laws she wants to obey and ignoring the laws she doesn't.[4]

I appreciate this is a difficult issue for many Christians. However, I do not wish to get embroiled in the question of which specific laws Christians should take from the Law of Moses. Instead, for our purposes in this book we will focus on the Ten Commandments. This is because the Ten Commandments are the 'high point' of God's moral law: they underpin everything else. In his book *Devoted to God*, Sinclair Ferguson outlines a few reasons why the Ten Commandments are distinct from the rest of the law:

> There the Decalogue [the Ten Commandments] is viewed as foundational to and distinct from its local and temporal applications. This distinction is built into the very way in which God gave the laws in the first place:
>
> - The Ten Commandments alone were spoken to the whole congregation.
>
> - The Ten Commandments alone were written on stone tablets.
>
> - The Ten Commandments alone were written by the finger of God.
>
> - The Ten Commandments alone were housed in the ark.
>
> By contrast,

---

[4] You can watch the scene on YouTube: https://youtu.be/Q5f_lUyfQUE

- The civil laws were given through Moses, not directly written by God.

- The civil laws and commands were to be kept while the people were 'in the land'.

- The ceremonial laws do not appear in the words of Deuteronomy which were spoken to the people as a whole – except insofar as they involved the people's action.[5]

So, the Ten Commandments were special. They cannot be dismissed simply as a part of the Law of Moses, along with e.g. the food purity laws. The Ten Commandments represented something fundamental about what God required of his people. This aligns with what Moses said in Deuteronomy 4:

He declared to you his covenant, the Ten Commandments, which he commanded you to follow and then wrote them on two stone tablets. And the Lord directed me at that time to teach you the decrees and laws you are to follow in the land that you are crossing the Jordan to possess.
Deuteronomy 4:13-14

The Ten Commandments are at the core of God's covenant, his relationship, with his people. The other laws from the Pentateuch (the civil and ceremonial laws) were given to a particular people at a particular time, to help them know how to obey God in that context. While they may give us insight today into what it means to obey the

---

[5] Sinclair Ferguson, *Devoted to God* (Kindle edition: 2016), 2614

commandments, they are not binding for Christians in the same way. (A happy thought for those of us who like to enjoy a bacon sandwich!)[6]

So, just why are the Ten Commandments so important? Let's think about why they were given in the first place.

Going back to the beginning

To answer that question, we need to go right back to the beginning. What was God's will for humanity from the start? We need to go back to the book of Genesis and the creation of the universe. This is what it says about the creation of mankind:

> So God created mankind in his own image,
>   in the image of God he created them;
>   male and female he created them.
> *Genesis 1:27*

This teaches us that human beings are made in the "image of God". This is the most fundamental truth the Bible teaches about humanity: each human being is precious because we are made in God's image and belong to him. There has been no single Christian doctrine which has had a greater impact on the Western world. This one verse has led to our views about equality, human rights, and so many other things we take for granted.[7]

---

[6] Of course, this is also simplifying the law – for example, the sacrificial laws, which have been fulfilled by Christ's sacrifice. See Sinclair Ferguson's book *Devoted to God* for a fuller explanation of the law.

[7] See Tom Holland's book *Dominion* for a thorough exploration of the way Christianity has impacted upon the modern world.

Let's think more deeply about what it means to be made in God's image. Christians have an insight into what God is like in a way that Old Testament believers did not. We have the doctrine of the Trinity, which was developed in the early years of the church as they wrestled with the question 'Who is Jesus?' One thing the Trinity means is that God is fundamentally *relational*. Mike Ovey, the late principal of my theological college, used to say: "The Trinity means that God is, from eternity, a community of other-person centred love."

If God is a community of love, and we are made in the image of God, does that not say something fundamental about humanity? Whatever else you may say about us as human beings, we are made to be part of a network of loving relationships. In the same way that you cannot define Jesus the Son of God without reference to the Father, you cannot define us as human beings without reference to our relationships. John Donne famously said, "No man is an island": our relationships are essential to who we are. You could say that *love* is at the core of who we are and how God wants us to live.

Sidebar: Men, women, and marriage

Have you ever considered before the significance of the creation of man and woman? Genesis 1:27, as we saw above, says that God created men and women equally in his image – you could say, that's the summary. But Genesis 2 gives us a little more detail.

We see Adam alone in the Garden of Eden, and this is the first time in Genesis where something is described as *not* good: "The Lord God said, 'It is not good for the man to be alone. I will make a helper suitable for him'" (Genesis 2:18). He then causes Adam to fall into a deep sleep, takes a rib from him, and creates Eve.

Then the narrator adds the note: "That is why a man leaves his father and mother and is united to his wife, and they become one flesh" (Genesis 2:24).

It would be easy to skim over this, yet it's a deeply significant truth. God has taken *one* man, formed *two* people (man and woman), and then in sexual union they become *one* again. One, becomes two, becomes one again.

This is why sexual intimacy is so fundamental – it's the high point of human love. It is where our love for one another finds its deepest physical expression. And for that reason, sexual ethics are very important in the Bible – simply because sex is so deep and powerful. We'll think more about this when we look at the commandments in Chapter Six.

How do the Ten Commandments fit in?

I'm sure you know that the perfect situation described at the beginning of the Bible (the first two chapters of Genesis) did not last long. In Genesis 3 sin enters the world, and Adam and Eve are expelled from the Garden of Eden. You can read for yourself what happens next in the book of Genesis – but we're going to skip on a little.

The Ten Commandments were given to God's people at Mount Sinai, once he had rescued them from slavery in Egypt[8]. Before we move on, it's extremely important to highlight this: God saved his people first, and only then gave them the law. This is the way it worked in the Old Testament, and it's the same with us as Christians: **God saves us first,**

---

[8] You might be familiar with some of the story from the musical *Joseph and the Amazing Technicolour Dreamcoat* and the film *Prince of Egypt* – but it's always better to read the source material!

then **calls us to a holy life**. Holiness is the *result* of salvation, not the requirement for it! We'll come back to this later.

What was the purpose of God giving the commandments? They were to teach his people how to obey him. This is how Sinclair Ferguson puts it:

> The law of God – in the sense of the Ten Commandments – was an expression of the will of God for the people he had delivered from bondage in Egypt. But in a deeper sense it gave expression to his original design for the lifestyle of men and women made in his image...

> The Ten Commandments therefore expressed, largely in negative terms (because addressed now to sinners), what God originally willed in a positive way for Adam and Eve in the Garden of Eden... There God was republishing his original blueprint for life.[9]

The Ten Commandments were not some new idea that God dreamt up for the Israelites at that moment. They were simply God "republishing his original blueprint for life": it was, in other words, nothing more than a statement of God's *original purpose for human beings* from the Garden of Eden. But, because people had become sinners and turned away from God, this changed the way the message was communicated. What they had previously known instinctively, they needed to be told explicitly in black-and-white.

This new context of sin also meant that God expressed his purposes differently. As Ferguson points out, the law was expressed largely in *negative* terms – i.e. "*Don't* do this or that". It made it easier for sinners to understand. But the underlying principles of love were exactly the

---

[9] *Devoted to God*, 2497

same as they were at creation. The only difference was how they were communicated, because of the different context.

The commandments in the New Testament

It's a common misconception that the Old Testament and the New Testament contain very different ideas about what God wants from us. This is the opposite of the truth: God's purposes remain consistent throughout the whole Bible. However, the vision of God's purposes for mankind in the commandments is made clearer in the New Testament. Let's look firstly at Jesus' explanation of the law:

> Hearing that Jesus had silenced the Sadducees, the Pharisees got together. One of them, an expert in the law, tested him with this question: 'Teacher, which is the greatest commandment in the Law?'
>
> Jesus replied: '"Love the Lord your God with all your heart and with all your soul and with all your mind." This is the first and greatest commandment. And the second is like it: "Love your neighbour as yourself." All the Law and the Prophets hang on these two commandments.'
> *Matthew 22:34-40*

Jesus condenses the whole law into just two commandments: to *love* the Lord your God, and to *love* your neighbour. He said that everything in the Law and the Prophets hung on those two commandments. This is completely logical given what we have seen about the Ten Commandments and God's purposes for humanity. Everything God wants from us is summed up in the one word, 'love'. We are to love others as God has loved from all eternity.

Further on in the New Testament, the apostle Paul builds on this understanding of the law:

> Let no debt remain outstanding, except the continuing debt to love one another, for whoever loves others has fulfilled the law. The commandments, 'You shall not commit adultery,' 'You shall not murder,' 'You shall not steal,' 'You shall not covet,' and whatever other command there may be, are summed up in this one command: 'Love your neighbour as yourself.' Love does no harm to a neighbour. Therefore love is the fulfilment of the law.
> *Romans 13:8-10*

Paul couldn't be clearer, could he? "Whoever loves others has fulfilled the law". It's there in black-and-white. But, for the avoidance of doubt, he spells it out in the next verse. He lists several of the commandments, then says they are "summed up in this one command: 'Love your neighbour…'". All the Ten Commandments are summed up in the *one* command to love. This is because, as he puts it, "love does no harm to a neighbour". In other words, **if we love others, we won't harm them**. Love and harm are opposites.

Let's summarise what we've learned so far.

The Ten Commandments and love

Everything that God wants from us as human beings can be summed up in the one word, 'love'. This is the way that he made us from the beginning. He wants us to love him, and he wants us to love our neighbour. The Ten Commandments are simply a *summary* of what that love should look like in our lives.

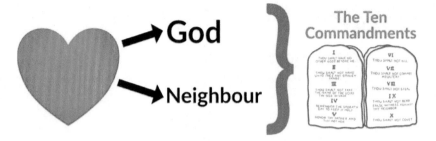

The commandments were given as an expression of God's purpose for us as human beings, to help sinful people understand what it meant to love God and love others in practice. It needed to be communicated differently (in negative terms) because it was given to sinners, but the purpose was still the same.

Now, at this point you might find yourself thinking, "why have we spent all this time on the purpose of the commandments? How does that help us to live as Christians?" Please be patient – we are trying to build the argument piece by piece. It is all necessary for our understanding, and you will see why as we go through.

In the next chapter we will look at the sad case of the Pharisees and see how misunderstanding the law leads to the wrong view about the Christian life.

Chapter Two: Love vs Pharisaism

The Pharisees and the law

In the previous chapter we saw how the Ten Commandments were an expression of God's purposes for humanity. He made human beings to love him and to love others: we are to be a community of other-person centred love, *just as God is*. That means love is at the core of who we are, and therefore **our relationships are essential.**

However, this isn't always the way that God's people have seen the law. In this chapter, we're going to think about what happens when you isolate the Ten Commandments from God's purposes of love. What would that do to your understanding of how we obey God?

As it happens, we don't need to guess. What I have just described is known as *Pharisaism*. This is a word coined from the group we read of in the Bible called the Pharisees. We don't know very much about them outside the Bible, but tradition has it that they were extremely zealous for the law. You could say they were *fanatical* about keeping the law.

To give you an idea of how fanatical they were, they had rules surrounding the commandments to prevent them from even going near breaking the law. For example, in the Ten Commandments God commanded the Israelites not to work on the Sabbath day. The Pharisees had rules about this to make sure that nothing you did on the Sabbath day constituted "work". For example, they were forbidden from picking and eating grain on the Sabbath (Mark 2:23-24). This was not part of God's law but an additional rule the Pharisees had created.

The Pharisees saw themselves as the squeakiest clean of the squeaky clean. They thought they were the ones who obeyed the law, unlike "sinners" such as Gentiles. In fact, the Pharisees didn't seem to see themselves as sinners at all – on the contrary, one gets the impression that some of the Pharisees thought God was lucky to have them. In the parable of the Pharisee and the Tax Collector, Jesus characterises the Pharisee like this:

> The Pharisee stood by himself and prayed: 'God, I thank you that I am not like other people – robbers, evildoers, adulterers – or even like this tax collector. I fast twice a week and give a tenth of all I get.'
> *Luke 18:11-12*

The Pharisees saw themselves as keepers of the law *par excellence*. In their own eyes they were virtuous, upright, and the moral superiors of just about everybody else – especially tax collectors. They considered their own law-keeping record to be spotless, so they didn't see themselves as needing salvation.

It will not come as a surprise to find that Jesus did not commend the Pharisees for their righteousness. If you've ever read the gospels, you'll know that they come in for some of Jesus' toughest criticism. Let's look at two examples from the gospels to help us understand how they'd managed to get it so wrong.

Sidebar: Pharisees or Teachers of the Law?

Jesus' criticisms are often not directed at the Pharisees alone, but also at the "teachers of the law". We don't know exactly who this group was, and it's not important for our purposes here. All we need to understand

25

is, when it came to the law, they saw eye-to-eye. They considered themselves to be righteous because of their superior obedience.

For the sake of simplicity, we will simply refer to this group as 'the Pharisees'.

Example #1: Commandment evasion

In Mark's Gospel, Jesus debates with the Pharisees and teachers of the law about what defiles – that is, what made them unclean[10]. They ask him why he and his disciples do not observe ceremonial hand washing – a tradition which had been invented by themselves, rather than given by God in the Scriptures (see Mark 7:1-8). Jesus responds that they are putting the traditions of man above the commands of God. He continues:

> 'You have a fine way of setting aside the commands of God in order to observe your own traditions! For Moses said, "Honour your father and mother," and, "Anyone who curses their father or mother is to be put to death." But you say that if anyone declares that what might have been used to help their father or mother is Corban (that is, devoted to God) – then you no longer let them do anything for their father or mother. Thus you nullify the word of God by your tradition that you have handed down. And you do many things like that.'
> Mark 7:9-13

---

[10] This refers to ceremonial cleanliness, not physical. Uncleanness was part of the Old Testament law where certain things such as some animals, illnesses, or contact with a dead body could make you ceremonially "unclean". The specifics are not important for our purposes here.

Here, we learn that the Pharisees would allow someone to set aside some money as "Corban" (devoted to God), which they would otherwise have used to help their parents. We are not given the details, but the result was they were excused from using the money to help their parents. This was despite the command, "Honour your father and mother". Presumably the Pharisees would have justified this by saying, since God was more important, he should take priority over their parents. It might have looked impressively pious to outsiders, but Jesus couldn't be fooled.

Jesus knew their hearts and what was going on under the surface. He knew that they declared money as "Corban" not from devotion to God, but from a love of money. The Pharisees had created "Corban" to be a kind of legal loophole so they could get out of their obligation to love their parents.

You can imagine the Corban advertising posters up in the temple (if they were honest): "Do you love money? Would you prefer to bank it instead of giving it to your parents for their care home? Simply designate the money as Corban, and all your obligations will disappear! Ask us about our Corban investment scheme…"

Why did the Pharisees get the commandments so wrong? The heart of their problem was that they saw the commandments as wooden, black-and-white rules, detached from love. They treated them as an opportunity to find creative ways of getting out of their duties, so they could indulge their selfish desires rather than love others. You've heard of tax evasion – this was commandment evasion! They could only do it because they didn't see love behind the commandments – and love is not something which should ever be evaded.

Example #2: Upside down priorities

Jesus also accused the Pharisees of getting their priorities wrong. In Matthew's gospel, Jesus pronounces seven "woes" on the teachers of the law and the Pharisees. Let's look at one of them:

> Woe to you, teachers of the law and Pharisees, you hypocrites! You give a tenth of your spices – mint, dill and cumin. But you have neglected the more important matters of the law – justice, mercy and faithfulness. You should have practised the latter, without neglecting the former. You blind guides! You strain out a gnat but swallow a camel.
> *Matthew 23:23-24*

In the law, the Israelites were required to give a tenth ("tithe") of their produce to God (Leviticus 27:30). Jesus says here that the Pharisees were obsessive about tithing – even to the point of tithing their garden spices! As we said earlier, they were *fanatical* about the letter of the law. But Jesus goes on to say they've got their priorities wrong: they had forgotten "the more important matters of the law", which he defines as "justice, mercy and faithfulness".

Jesus says, once again, that the Pharisees had seen the law only in wooden, black-and-white terms: they had isolated the command from the bigger picture of love. Jesus brings them back to reality and says they are missing the fundamental purpose of the law. He uses one of his most famous and memorable images to describe what they are doing – "straining out a gnat but swallowing a camel". What an indictment!

Sometimes people talk about the difference between the letter of the law and the spirit of the law. The Pharisees were obsessive about keeping the letter of the law but paid no attention to the spirit of the law. They had got things totally backwards.

What Jesus taught about the law

In the Sermon on the Mount, Jesus devotes an extended section of teaching to the law. This is the most concentrated section of teaching from Jesus himself on how we should understand the law, and as such it's important for us to look at. Doubly so in this chapter, because much of it starts with the Pharisees' misconceptions about the law.

We won't go through the whole section (you can read it all for yourself in Matthew 5:17-48), but we will look at a couple of extracts. Jesus starts out by speaking positively about the law:

> Do not think that I have come to abolish the Law or the Prophets; I have not come to abolish them but to fulfil them. For truly I tell you, until heaven and earth disappear, not the smallest letter, not the least stroke of a pen, will by any means disappear from the Law until everything is accomplished. Therefore anyone who sets aside one of the least of these commands and teaches others accordingly will be called least in the kingdom of heaven, but whoever practises and teaches these commands will be called great in the kingdom of heaven. For I tell you that unless your righteousness surpasses that of the Pharisees and the teachers of the law, you will certainly not enter the kingdom of heaven.
> *Matthew 5:17-20*

Jesus says he came not to *abolish* the law or the prophets but to *fulfil* them. He also said that "not the least stroke of a pen" would disappear from the law until everything was accomplished. Jesus made very clear that he was in no way abrogating the law or reducing its demands. In fact, quite the opposite: he says that our righteousness needs to *surpass* that of the Pharisees to enter the kingdom of heaven. As we saw at the start of this chapter, the Pharisees saw themselves as keepers of the law *par excellence*. Jesus was saying that **we don't need less obedience than the Pharisees, but more**. We will not enter the Kingdom of Heaven unless we are more righteous than they were.

How is it possible for us to be more righteous than the Pharisees without becoming an even bigger Pharisee? The answer lies in the way the Pharisees misunderstood the law – as we've already seen in this chapter. This is exactly what Jesus goes on to say. He gives several examples of where the law had been misunderstood, but we will look at just one:

> You have heard that it was said, "Love your neighbour and hate your enemy." But I tell you, love your enemies and pray for those who persecute you, that you may be children of your Father in heaven. He causes his sun to rise on the evil and the good, and sends rain on the righteous and the unrighteous. If you love those who love you, what reward will you get? Are not even the tax collectors doing that? And if you greet only your own people, what are you doing more than others? Do not even pagans do that? Be perfect, therefore, as your heavenly Father is perfect.
> *Matthew 5:43-48*

Jesus starts out by quoting a command, "Love your neighbour and hate your enemy". If you were paying attention in Chapter One, you will notice a crucial difference to the law which God gave. The Pharisees had tacked on the last four words about hating your enemy. They had added to the law, to 'clarify' it.

They were saying that the command to love your neighbour only applied to a friend – it didn't apply to 'enemies'. Once again, they had created a loophole to get out of obeying the law when it was inconvenient or difficult for them. But, Jesus says, we should set our sights higher and be like our Father in heaven. We should have higher standards than those of this world: as he points out, even tax collectors love people who love them. It's not hard to love people who love us. But Jesus says the standard of love we should be aiming for is that of our Father in heaven, who loves even his enemies.

We mustn't let ourselves off the hook by creating loopholes in the law. We mustn't add to the law to 'clarify' it. Instead, we should fix our eyes on God's love which gives life and meaning to the law. As Jesus says, "Be perfect, therefore, as your heavenly father is perfect."

If we really understood these words, they should send a chill through our hearts: Jesus is literally telling us that the standard God requires is **nothing short of perfection**. No ifs, no buts, no loopholes or clarifications or excuses. We should love God and love our neighbour, with our whole hearts, one hundred per cent of the time.

If you find that a scary thought, don't worry – that is exactly what Jesus intended. No-one should be thinking, "well, that sounds pretty easy". That's the whole point. Jesus didn't intend to make things easy for us. His intention was that we need to fulfil the whole law of love, the law which lies *behind* the Ten Commandments. That is why he came.

How far short do we fall?

Because the Pharisees didn't see the law of love behind the Ten Commandments, they had a hugely distorted view of themselves: they simply didn't realise how sinful they were. In fact, as we saw at the start, they hardly thought of themselves as sinners at all! They thought that their obedience was exemplary because in their own eyes they obeyed every one of the Ten Commandments perfectly.

They saw themselves as 'top of the class': they had achieved perfect righteousness by obeying the law through their own efforts.

However, that was not Jesus' view. He saw that they, just like everyone else, did not live up to God's standards of love. The Pharisees were, therefore, **utterly blind to their own condition**. They did not understand themselves, because they judged themselves to be righteous.

God's standards of obedience *(Love & 10 C's)*
How well the Pharisees *thought* they kept the law
How well they kept the law in reality

0% --- 100%

The effect of Pharisaism

What effect do you think having such a distorted view of yourself might have on your attitude towards God and other people? The effect is demonstrated clearly in this episode from Luke's Gospel.

> When one of the Pharisees invited Jesus to have dinner with him, he went to the Pharisee's house and reclined at the table. A woman in that town who lived a sinful life learned that Jesus was eating at the Pharisee's house, so she came there with an alabaster

jar of perfume. As she stood behind him at his feet weeping, she began to wet his feet with her tears. Then she wiped them with her hair, kissed them and poured perfume on them.

When the Pharisee who had invited him saw this, he said to himself, "If this man were a prophet, he would know who is touching him and what kind of woman she is — that she is a sinner."

Jesus answered him, "Simon, I have something to tell you."

"Tell me, teacher," he said.

"Two people owed money to a certain moneylender. One owed him five hundred denarii, and the other fifty. Neither of them had the money to pay him back, so he forgave the debts of both. Now which of them will love him more?"

Simon replied, "I suppose the one who had the bigger debt forgiven."

"You have judged correctly," Jesus said.

Then he turned toward the woman and said to Simon, "Do you see this woman? I came into your house. You did not give me any water for my feet, but she wet my feet with her tears and wiped them with her hair. You did not give me a kiss, but this woman, from the time I entered, has not stopped kissing my feet. You did not put oil on my head, but she has poured perfume on my feet. Therefore, I tell you, her many sins have been forgiven — as her great love has shown. But whoever has been forgiven little loves little."

Then Jesus said to her, "Your sins are forgiven."

The other guests began to say among themselves, "Who is this who even forgives sins?"

Jesus said to the woman, "Your faith has saved you; go in peace."
Luke 7:36-50

The heart of this account is the contrast between two people: a Pharisee named Simon, and an unnamed "sinful woman". We already know what the Pharisees thought of themselves, but what do we know of the sinful woman?

Luke gives us very little information about her, leaving the identity of the woman (and the details of her sinful life) to our imagination. Why? Because it means the only thing we know about her is that she was a *sinner*. The specifics of her sin (e.g., many speculate that she was a prostitute) are not relevant. The key point for us is that she stands for anyone who knows their own sinfulness – in other words, **it could be any one of us.**

Luke focusses us on the way Simon the Pharisee and the sinful woman relate to Jesus. It couldn't be more different: look at the contrasts that Jesus names in vv44-46:

Simon the Pharisee	Sinful woman
Did not give Jesus water	Wet Jesus' feet with her tears and wiped them with her hair
Did not give Jesus a kiss	Did not stop kissing Jesus' feet
Did not put oil on Jesus' head	Poured perfume on Jesus' feet

There is some debate among Biblical scholars as to whether Simon *deliberately* withheld those things as a snub to Jesus. In those days (as today), some things were considered basic politeness and others were not. For example, if we were hosting a guest for dinner it would be rude not to take their coat, but they probably wouldn't expect a foot massage. The upshot is, we can't say for sure whether Simon was being deliberately rude, or whether he was simply providing the minimum needed to be polite.

Either way, it doesn't affect the difference between them. The contrast between the two responses to Jesus is crystal clear: the sinful woman treated Jesus with a genuine love and respect which Simon did not. Simon did not go out of his way to welcome his guest – and possibly even snubbed him. By contrast, the woman poured out her love on him, not caring about what anyone else would think of her.

The key question is, why did they behave so differently? This is what Jesus' mini parable in the middle is about. He asks Simon who would love more – someone who had a small debt cancelled, or someone who had a large debt cancelled. The point Jesus was making is simple: someone who has been forgiven a lot will love a lot.

Jesus says this explains why the sinful woman was so full of love to him, whereas Simon showed him very little love. The sinful woman knew the value of forgiveness – she knew how little she deserved it, and how much difference it had made in her life. She was full of love for the forgiveness she had been shown. Simon the Pharisee, on the other hand, believing that he was a rule-keeper *par excellence*, didn't think he needed forgiveness. He couldn't show gratitude for what he thought he didn't need!

The message here is striking. The ones whom Jesus commends are those who know their own sinfulness. They know how sinful they are and consequently how much they need to be forgiven. By contrast, those who think they are good enough already simply don't understand what

God requires of us – and they have very little love. They come under harsh criticism from Jesus.

Pharisaism is all about "me"

The problem with the Pharisees was not simply that they lacked love, but that they loved themselves more than anything. One of the most tragic things about the Pharisees is that an obsession with keeping the rules led to them being incredibly self-centred. One has to wonder, who did they think they were benefitting by keeping the rules? It certainly wasn't other people!

And this is one of the worst problems with a rule-keeping obsession: instead of considering what is best for others, we end up considering what is best for ourselves. The Pharisees were obsessed with the law, yet they showed little concern for others. They demonstrated that their rule-keeping was only about feeding their own sense of moral self-righteousness.

This is perhaps the darkest and most insidious effect of Pharisaism: we end up focussed on ourselves and our own performance. This is the very opposite of the way God wants us to be. We will think more about this in the next chapter.

Why the Pharisees would never succeed

There is a reason why the Pharisees would never have succeeded, however hard they tried. The problem of the Pharisees was misunderstanding what sin was all about. The Pharisees thought sin was all about our *behaviour*: it was something which could be controlled by following a few simple rules. (Or, more accurately, a mass of bewilderingly complex rules!) But, Jesus says, the problem was far deeper than that. Straight after the passage we looked at in the first example ("Commandment evasion"), Jesus goes on to say this:

> Again Jesus called the crowd to him and said, "Listen to me, everyone, and understand this. Nothing outside a person can defile them by going into them. Rather, it is what comes out of a person that defiles them."
>
> … He went on: "What comes out of a person is what defiles them. For it is from within, out of a person's heart, that evil thoughts come – sexual immorality, theft, murder, adultery, greed, malice, deceit, lewdness, envy, slander, arrogance and folly. All these evils come from inside and defile a person."
> *Mark 7:14-15, 20-23*

If you think sin is all about our behaviour, and all we need to do is avoid doing certain bad things, you'll think the solution is to put rules in place so you can avoid doing those bad things. But Jesus says this is not how it works. He says that sin comes "out of a person's heart". In other words, we only *do* the wrong things because we *want* the wrong things – our desires are what lead to our sinful behaviour.

Keeping laws, even as fanatically as the Pharisees, could never deal with the problem of wanting bad things. This is why Jesus said to them:

> Woe to you, teachers of the law and Pharisees, you hypocrites! You are like whitewashed tombs, which look beautiful on the outside but on the inside are full of the bones of the dead and everything unclean.
> *Matthew 23:27*

The Pharisees were like "whitewashed tombs" – they looked righteous on the outside, but they were deeply unrighteous on the inside. They liked to think of themselves as above reproach, but the inner reality was almost the complete opposite. Beneath their righteous appearance, their hearts were filled with sinfulness. This is the problem with Pharisaism in a nutshell.

Jesus says that the solution to the problem of our hearts is not more rules and regulation. We need something radically different. That's why the Pharisees failed – their solution fell far short of making a difference in the one place it was really needed.

It's sobering to think that the ones who considered themselves to be the most righteous in the gospels are the ones who conspired together to kill the Son of God. They were righteous in their own eyes, but they had very little love – and so they thought nothing of killing an innocent man. As we come to the end of this chapter, take a moment to reflect on just how the 'righteous' can get it so badly wrong. And then ask God to help you have a right understanding of yourself.

Chapter Three: How sinful are we really?

I'm not *that* bad, surely...

In the previous chapter, we examined what happens when you begin to see God's commands without the love behind them. This is what happened to the Pharisees. They ended up with a totally distorted view of themselves, to the point of not thinking of themselves as sinners at all. But what relevance does this have to us now – we're not Pharisees, are we?

Today, although most people are aware they're not perfect, they don't think of themselves as sinners. A few years ago, our church ran an Alpha course. One evening, during the group discussion after watching the video, we were talking about what it meant to sin and be sinners. A woman in my group commented, "Well, I do curse occasionally..." as if the worst sin she thought she committed was swearing from time to time! She wasn't saying she was perfect, or close to it – she just didn't think of herself as a sinner in any meaningful sense.

I suspect that most people, if they were honest with themselves, would say something similar: not perfect, for sure, but not *that* bad. They may slip up and make a "mistake" from time to time – but they are fundamentally good people who occasionally do something wrong.

This is a huge barrier to understanding the good news of Jesus Christ. C.S. Lewis once wrote:

> The greatest barrier I have met is the almost total absence from the minds of my audience of any sense of sin... The early Christian preachers could assume in their hearers, whether Jews, Metuentes, or Pagans, a sense of guilt. (That this was common among Pagans is shown by the fact that both Epicureanism and the mystery religions both claimed, though in different ways, to assuage it.) Thus the Christian message was in those days unmistakably the Evangelium, the Good News. It promised healing to those who knew they were sick. We have to convince our hearers of the unwelcome diagnosis before we can expect them to welcome the news of the remedy.[11]

Lewis points out that we need to understand the *sickness* before we can truly understand the *remedy*. If we don't understand how sick we are, we won't look for the right cure – and if we don't think we're sick at all, we won't even know that we need a cure! Jesus said: "It is not the healthy who need a doctor, but the sick. I have not come to call the righteous, but sinners to repentance" (Luke 5:31-32).

In this chapter, we're going to examine what the Scriptures have to say about our sickness. How big a problem is sin, really? We're going to begin by thinking about why we need saving in the first place.

---

[11] C.S. Lewis, *God in the Dock*, see online:
https://www.goodreads.com/quotes/552967-the-greatest-barrier-i-have-met-is-the-almost-total

The gap between good and evil

Queen Elizabeth II said in her 2011 Christmas Day broadcast:

> Although we are capable of great acts of kindness, history teaches us that we sometimes need saving from ourselves - from our recklessness or our greed.
>
> God sent into the world a unique person - neither a philosopher nor a general, important though they are, but a Saviour, with the power to forgive.[12]

I'm sure that most people would agree with the Queen that human recklessness and greed have caused, and continue to cause, many problems throughout history. We do not need to be convinced that there are deep problems with humanity in places. There have been some very evil people, and every day the news has stories of wicked things which people have done.

But does the word "evil" apply only to some people, and not to others? The Queen made the point that we need saving. The question which we must ask is, do we all need saving *equally?* Are we, as a human race, basically good with only a few bad apples, or are we more alike than we realise?

Perhaps an illustration will help. Think about this question: how big a difference is there between the very worst human being – let's say for the sake of argument, Adolf Hitler – and the very best human being, let's say Mother Teresa?

---

[12] See online: https://www.bbc.co.uk/news/uk-16328899

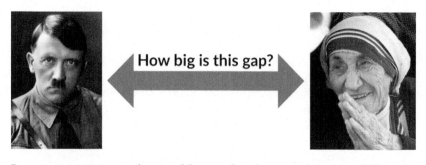

I suspect most people would say there's an enormous difference between these two people: Hitler is widely considered one of the most evil men who ever lived, whereas Mother Teresa is hailed as a saint who dedicated her life to helping the sick in Calcutta.

Let's take this illustration one step further. If there was a line from 100% good to 100% evil, where would you put Hitler, Mother Teresa, and yourself? I am sure we would agree that no-one is 100% good or 100% evil. We're all a mixture, but perhaps we see people as 'mostly' bad or 'mostly' good.

I expect most of us would put ourselves somewhere in the dotted area – between the extremes of Hitler and Mother Teresa. But probably closer to Mother Teresa! That's how we like to think of ourselves, isn't it? Maybe we're not saints, but we're not evil!

However, as we saw with the Pharisees, the key thing is not what we think of ourselves but what God thinks about us. His diagnosis of our condition is the only thing which really matters. So, what do the Scriptures have to say about sin and our humanity? Let's consider what Jesus had to say.

Are we good or bad?

Consider this brief exchange from Mark's Gospel:

> As Jesus started on his way, a man ran up to him and fell on his knees before him. "Good teacher," he asked, "what must I do to inherit eternal life?"
>
> "Why do you call me good?" Jesus answered. "No one is good — except God alone.
> *Mark 10:17-18*

Jesus rarely gave a straight answer to a question, which is exactly what we see here. As the man comes to Jesus, he calls him "Good teacher". Jesus picks him up on this and asks why he calls him good. He adds, "No one is good – except God alone".

Let's think about this for a moment. You and I may use the word "good" casually: we very easily categorise people as good or bad. It seems like basic common sense, doesn't it? But Jesus says that we need to think a bit more carefully about what we're saying. In fact, Jesus says, only God can *truly* be called good.

How can that be so? The point Jesus is making is that to be "good" is to achieve pure, unadulterated goodness. Someone cannot be called good if they are, say, 50% good. A mixture of good and bad is not "good". For something to truly be good it must be pure, undiluted goodness.

So, if we are not good, what are we instead? Again, two quotes from Jesus' lips:

> The world cannot hate you, but it hates me because I testify that its works are evil.
> *John 7:7*

> If you, then, though you are evil, know how to give good gifts to your children, how much more will your Father in heaven give good gifts to those who ask him!
> *Matthew 7:11*

Take a moment to read those sentences again: I don't want you to miss the force of what Jesus is saying. There's a word which Jesus uses in both to describe us, and that word is **evil**.

Ouch! How many of us would feel comfortable using that word to describe our friends, colleagues, family members, or neighbours? When we think of evil, we probably think of people like Pol Pot and Hitler, or movie villains and the like. And yet Jesus, the Son of God, who knows us more deeply than we know ourselves, calls us evil.

How could Jesus say such a thing? Jesus was (and is) the most loving person who ever lived. I am writing this paragraph as we approach Christmas, and the words of *Silent Night* are ringing in my ears:

> Silent Night! Holy Night!
> Son of God, Love's pure light...

Jesus was indeed the Son of God, Love's pure light. And yet, he did not hold back from calling the world "evil". In order to understand what he meant, we need to do some thinking about what good and evil actually are.

What is good and evil?

We tend to think of evil as meaning 'something very bad', which is the way most people use the word. Hitler was "evil" because he was an *extremely* bad man, and so on. We reserve the word for the very worst people and deeds. It might come as a shock, therefore, to see that's not how the Bible uses the word.

As we saw back in the first chapter, the whole of the law can be summed up in the one word 'love': love for God, and love for neighbour. The definition of good, therefore, is to love. Consequently, the definition of evil is linked to the definition of good – they are opposites. It will help us to understand what evil is if we think more deeply about love.

Love is something which it is easier to sing about than define. You will often hear pop songs about love, but they are usually talking about romance. Surely love is bigger than that: we have love for our parents, love for children, love for friends, love for our fellow man – love is far bigger than romance.

Fortunately, the Bible does help us out here as well:

> This is how we know what love is: Jesus Christ laid down his life for us. And we ought to lay down our lives for our brothers and sisters.
> *1 John 3:16*

The apostle John tells us that we *do* have a way of knowing what love is. It is Jesus Christ, and specifically, Jesus Christ laying down his life for us.

How does that help us to define love? It means we can say that love involves two things:

PHILL SACRE

1. Setting aside one's own preferences – even to the point of our own lives…
2. … so that we might bring good to another.

Love involves putting others first and seeking THEIR good rather than our own. There is no greater model of that than the Lord Jesus, who sacrificed his own life for us so that we might live. He said, "Greater love has no one than this: to lay down one's life for one's friends" (John 15:13). That is exactly what he did for us – showed us the greatest love that it's possible to show.

But Jesus didn't only demonstrate his love by sacrificing himself – he demonstrated it by his life as well. If you want to see what love looks like in action, look no further than the pages of the gospels. Jesus loved with everything he did. It was *all* for the good of others. He healed them, he taught them, he rebuked them, he laughed with them, he cried with them. Absolutely everything in his life and death was done in love.

Let's pause for a moment and think about what that means for ourselves. As we saw at the start of this chapter, we often think that we're pretty good. However, this is only because we compare ourselves with other people. But what if we compare ourselves with Jesus instead – Jesus, who shows us what love really looks like? If God asks us to love others, and Jesus showed us what love looks like, then surely comparing ourselves with him is the only thing which will reveal the truth.

So, how do you stack up against Jesus? My guess is that you will look the same as me: compared with Jesus, I look very bad indeed.

Evil is love gone wrong

We have established that love is about doing what is right and good for others – even to the point of laying down our own lives. That is true love which we see demonstrated in Jesus. So, how does that help us to define evil? This is where we need the insights of Martin Luther, the famous Reformation theologian. In this passage he is building on a theologian of the early church called Augustine. Luther said:

> Scripture describes man as so curved in upon himself that he uses not only physical but even spiritual goods for his own purposes and in all things seeks only himself.[13]

The phrase "curved in upon himself" is deeply significant. It means that we have become focussed in upon our own interests and desires. Rather than loving God and loving our neighbour, our love is directed back to ourselves:

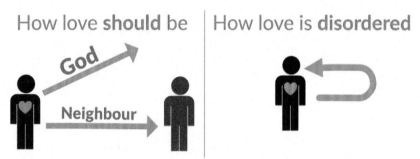

How love **should** be | How love is **disordered**

God

Neighbour

The problem with our love is not that we don't love *at all* – but that we love the wrong things. Instead of loving and worshipping God, we love and worship idols of our own choosing. Instead of laying down our own

---

[13] Quoted online: https://mbird.com/glossary/incurvatus-in-se/

lives to serve our neighbours, we use other people to serve our own interests. You could say **evil is love which has gone wrong.**

And here is the really sneaky thing: disordered self-love can *look like* real love. It masquerades as real love, it may even feel a bit like it sometimes, but it's not the real deal. Everything that we do is tainted by this disordered self-love – even the 'best' things that we do. Let me try to demonstrate.

Take a moment to recall the best good deed you've ever done. Maybe you helped a friend who was in need. Maybe you gave a big donation to charity. Maybe you were kind to someone who didn't deserve it.

Once you have something in mind, be completely honest with yourself: in that moment, were you acting *purely* out of love for the person or people involved? Or was there an element of self-love in there? Were you thinking, for example, "This will make me feel good"? Or, "This will ease my conscience?" Or, "Other people will think I'm a good person?"

The point I am making is that even our very best deeds fall short of God's perfect standards of love. Even the most selfless acts are still in some way corrupted by disordered self-love. If that's the case for our best deeds, how do you think we do the rest of the time?

It's not a pleasant thought, is it?

When you really start thinking about it, you realise that **none** of our good deeds are truly good deeds. We never do something truly good, because everything is corrupted with disordered self-love: we do things at least partially from selfish motives, rather than pure motives. The troubling implication is that you and I have **never done a good deed in our whole lives**. You and I, and every human being who has ever lived (except for Jesus), have *never* done a truly good deed.

This is the reason Jesus said that we are "evil": it's because we have never done anything which is truly good. If you take a cup of water and add even a drop of poison to it, it becomes poison. It's like that with disordered self-love: disordered love poisons and pollutes any real love that we have and ends up becoming evil.

That doesn't mean everything we do is equally bad – murder is worse than anger, for example. Stealing someone's car is worse than feeling jealous of it. The point is the two things are still evil – even if they are not equally bad.

We started out this chapter by posing the question, "How sinful are we really?". What we've seen is that we are sinful almost beyond comprehension. Rather than being good people who do the right thing most of the time but who occasionally sin, we sin *all the time*. That's because we do not do things out of love for God or love for our neighbour, but rather we are motivated (at least in part) by disordered self-love.

One of the reasons it's important to understand this is that it helps us to recognise that sin is not just about what we do, but what we *don't* do. If I actively harm someone that is obviously not loving them. However, I can also show a lack of love by ignoring them when they need me to help them.

If I don't do the good I know I should do, that is sin just as much as doing the wrong I shouldn't do. James 4:17 says, "If anyone, then, knows the good they ought to do and doesn't do it, it is sin for them." Failing to do good is just as much sin as actively doing wrong.

We are going to finish this chapter by thinking about how this helps us to start making sense of the Christian life.

Sin is not just what we do

In my experience, the way most people think of sin is like one of those old car-racing arcade games where you had to get around the track without hitting anything. It's all about *avoiding the obstacles*. It's like that with Christianity: we think that the Christian life  is about getting through life without sinning, so we avoid doing bad things.

This is exactly what the Pharisees tried to do. They added lots of extra rules around the commandments to prevent them even getting close to sinning. (Although, as we have seen, they also added things to the commandments to make it much easier for themselves). To take this to its logical conclusion, it would mean avoiding other people completely from fear of sinning.

However, if we recognise that God calls us to love, and the problem with us is disordered self-love, we will recognise that **the sins we *don't* do are just as important – probably more important – than the sins we *do*.**

The Protestant reformers of the 16th century came to recognise the importance of this truth. For example, let me quote one of the confessions from the Church of England's Book of Common Prayer. This is how it begins:

> Almighty and most merciful Father,
> We have erred, and strayed from thy ways like lost sheep,
> We have followed too much the devices and desires of our own hearts,
> We have offended against thy holy laws,

We have left undone those things which we ought to have done,
And we have done those things which we ought not to have
done,
And there is no health in us

Note that the confession includes the words "we have left undone those things which we ought to have done" first. The confession recognises that it is right and important to repent of the ways that we have sinned by not doing what is right, as well as actively doing what is wrong. Theologians call these sins of *omission* and *commission*: commission = active wrongdoing, omission = things we fail to do. In this confession we acknowledge that we are guilty of both.

It goes on to say, "there is no health in us". This means that we do not have a store of good deeds which we can offer to God to show our merits and earn our salvation. We have been so completely corrupted by sin that we need his forgiveness and healing in everything. Every good thing about us has been in some way infected by the disease of disordered self-love.

The good news of the gospel is that we have a Saviour who is capable of cleansing and restoring us completely. We do not need forgiveness for a few bad deeds here and there; we need a complete renewal. And this is *exactly what Jesus offers*. He can forgive us, heal us, and give us new hearts that begin to beat with love.

There is a wonderful promise which God gave in the Old Testament through the prophet Ezekiel:

I will sprinkle clean water on you, and you will be clean; I will cleanse you from all your impurities and from all your idols. I will give you a new heart and put a new spirit in you; I will remove from you your heart of stone and give you a heart of

flesh. And I will put my Spirit in you and move you to follow my decrees and be careful to keep my laws.
Ezekiel 36:25-27

God promised to cleanse us and give us new hearts, and we need nothing less. Not simply forgiving us and setting us back on our feet to try again, but a complete transformation. And when God transforms us, we can start not simply to avoid doing bad things, but to act from a genuine love for others. That's what we are going to turn to in the next chapter as we study the book of Galatians.

Chapter Four: Galatians on sin, grace, and holy living

Why is Galatians so important?

In my opinion, there is no book in the Bible which surpasses Galatians for setting out the relationship between the law, grace, and a holy life. In this one short letter, Paul sets down everything that we need to know.

Galatians was written by Paul the apostle, sometime around 50AD – it was likely one of the first books in the New Testament to be written. Biblical scholar Merrill Tenney called it "The Charter of Christian Liberty". It was a cornerstone of the Reformation – in fact, Martin Luther said of it: "The Epistle to the Galatians is my epistle. To it I am as it were in wedlock. It is my Katherine [Katherine was the name of Luther's wife]."[14] High praise indeed!

In this chapter, we are going to study the book of Galatians to draw out what Paul has to say about the Christian life. We won't go through the whole book in equal depth, but we will pick out a few key passages. In particular, we are going to focus in some detail on chapter five, where

---

[14] See online: https://www.ccel.org/ccel/luther/galatians.ii.html

Paul lays out the *how* of the Christian life. We will look more briefly at the first few chapters.

> **Explore Further:** Much of the material here I have drawn from preaching through Galatians. If you would like to explore further, the sermons are all available online – this includes the whole book, not just a few passages.[15]

Context

Before we get into studying Galatians, we need to set the scene and understand what caused Paul to write the letter in the first place. This will form the backdrop for our study.

The first thing to note is that this letter was written to a new church in the Roman province of Galatia. (Of course, *all* churches would have been new at that time!). Christianity began as a Jewish movement, but quickly spread to include Gentiles as well. Galatia was an ethnically mixed area, and we know that "throughout the region the church was predominantly Gentile."[16]

The reason Paul wrote to the church was because the church was being thrown into "confusion" (Galatians 5:10). The church had been established by Paul and Barnabas, but after they left some others arrived:

> After Paul and Barnabas had left the scene, apparently some Jewish Christians came into the area and taught that those who

---

[15] You can find them on YouTube via the Understand the Bible website – see this page: https://understandthebible.uk/tags/bible-galatians/
[16] Moo and Carson, *An Introduction to the New Testament, 2nd Edition* (Nottingham: Apollos, 2005), 465

embrace the Christian salvation must submit to the Jewish law, the Torah ... Their emphasis on keeping the Mosaic law makes it almost certain they were Jews.[17]

In those days, Jews believed that they were superior to the Gentiles because God had given them the law. Because Gentiles did not have the law, they were considered "sinners". It was only natural that some Jewish Christians would be confused about whether they needed to keep the law or not – especially whether Gentile converts needed to effectively become Jewish and keep the whole Law of Moses.[18]

So, the church was conflicted about grace and the law: they had started out by believing Paul's message of grace, but they were being thrown into confusion by a group of Jewish Christians who taught that they must keep the Law of Moses in order to be saved (including things such as circumcision – Galatians 5:3).

These Jewish Christians – and we should note that Paul calls into question whether they are Christians or not – were attacking Paul. They questioned his authority (which is why he starts out by defending his apostolic authority), they criticised his attitude to the law, and they criticised his gospel for leading to immoral living. It is in this context that Paul outlines how grace will lead to moral living in a way that the law could never do.

---

[17] Ibid, 465

[18] The idea that Gentiles need to keep the whole Law of Moses is explicitly rejected in the Council of Jerusalem, which we read about in Acts 15. The fact that Paul does not refer to this in Galatians, when it would have been hugely helpful for his case, suggests the letter was written before the events described in Acts 15.

I hope that you can see from this brief introduction how the letter will be helpful to us: although our circumstances are different, we do want to discover exactly what a Christian's relationship with the law should be, and how that should lead to living a life of obedience to God. How does grace lead to a holy life?

We will discover Paul's answer to these questions as we go.

Introduction (1:1-5)

Our first stop in this tour through Galatians is the introduction. Many people skim over the introductory words to a New Testament letter, but they usually summarise what is to come and introduce important concepts. Galatians is no exception.

After Paul introduces himself, he says: "Grace and peace to you from God our Father and the Lord Jesus Christ." Paul starts out with grace and peace. These words are Paul's summary of the message that he is going to expand on through the letter.

What is the heart of that message of grace and peace? He goes on: "who gave himself for our sins to rescue us from the present evil age." The atonement – that is, Christ's sacrificial death on the cross for us, to take away our sins – is at the heart of Paul's message. Through Christ we receive God's grace, and this means we have peace with God.

Notice that Paul includes the purpose of Jesus dying for our sins: it was "to rescue us from the present evil age". Paul describes this age as "evil" (see what we said about evil in Chapter Three). Christians, by contrast, are rescued from it. The implication is that we are no longer to participate in evil, instead our goal should be to live a life of righteousness.

So, right here in the introduction, we have been given the message: through the cross, Jesus Christ has rescued us from our sins and the evil of this world and called us to live a holy life. That's the message which Paul is going to elaborate on in the rest of the letter.

How we are justified (2:15-21)

You might have heard of the word "justification" before, but do you know what it means? To be justified is to be made right with God, to be accounted righteous before him. It means that, despite our sinfulness, God considers us righteous because of Jesus Christ.

You may know that justification was a key debate during the 16th century Reformation. The biggest question at that time was – do we play any part in our own justification? Are we justified because we in some way deserve it through our inherent goodness or obedience to the law? Or, are we justified solely on the basis of faith in Christ? This is why reformers such as Martin Luther loved Galatians so much – because it speaks so clearly about justification.

The Jewish Christians (who we met in the introduction) were teaching that being justified involved obeying the law. They said that it wasn't enough simply to have faith in Christ – one must basically become Jewish and obey the whole law to be saved.

With that in mind, let's dive into how Paul responds here.

> We who are Jews by birth and not sinful Gentiles know that a person is not justified by the works of the law, but by faith in Jesus Christ, So we, too, have put our faith in Christ Jesus that we may be justified by faith in Christ and not by the works of the

law, because by the works of the law no one will be justified. (2:15-16)

Paul starts out by contrasting "we who are Jews by birth" with "sinful Gentiles". When he uses the word "sinful", it should have quotes round it. Paul is simply saying what Jews at that time *thought* of the Gentiles. He is not saying that the Gentiles really were the sinful ones, otherwise that would undermine his whole argument.

He goes on: "a person is not justified by the works of the law, but by faith in Jesus Christ." Paul says that Jews need to be justified by faith in Jesus Christ, *just as much as Gentiles do*. They need Jesus equally, whether they have the law or not.

Why is that? "Because by the works of the law no one will be justified". As we saw in Chapter Three, none of us keep the law perfectly – in fact, we fall short of keeping the law at every point. If the standard required to be justified by the law is perfect obedience, then *no one* can be justified! At least, not in our own strength. Not the Jews, not the Gentiles, not anybody. This is exactly Paul's point here – all of humanity is in the same boat together.

> But if, in seeking to be justified in Christ, we Jews find ourselves also among the sinners, doesn't that mean that Christ promotes sin? Absolutely not! If I rebuild what I destroyed, then I really would be a law-breaker. (2:17-18)

Here, Paul is responding to a criticism from the Jewish Christians: if we are all justified equally by faith in Christ, doesn't that make the Jews "sinners"? And doesn't that mean that Christ promotes sin – by making people sinners? Paul responds very decisively here – "Absolutely not" (which is a very strong phrase, translated in the King James Version as

"God forbid!"). Christ came to *save* us from our sins – how could he make us sinners?

Paul explains, "If I rebuild what I destroyed, then I really would be a law-breaker." He means that if he went back to trying to be justified by the law (as the Jewish Christians were advocating), that really would make him a "law-breaker". The law had already proven him once to be in the wrong. If he went back to the law again then surely the same verdict applies! Why would anyone do that? – it would be madness!

The final paragraph here is the crux of his argument:

> 'For through the law I died to the law so that I might live for God. I have been crucified with Christ and I no longer live, but Christ lives in me. The life I now live in the body, I live by faith in the Son of God, who loved me and gave himself for me. I do not set aside the grace of God, for if righteousness could be gained through the law, Christ died for nothing!' (2:19-21)

For Paul, this is the heart of the gospel message.

He starts out by saying "through the law I died to the law so that I might live for God." You could paraphrase this, in the words of *The Clash*, "I fought the law and the law won." The law did not give him life, it brought death. The law did not justify him, it exposed his sinfulness – his lack of love for God and neighbour.

And the solution was not trying harder to keep the law but *dying* to the law and then *living* to God. Dying and then living – death and resurrection. This is why he goes on to say: "I have been crucified with Christ and I no longer live, but Christ lives in me." Paul says he has *died* with Christ, and now he is alive through Christ living in him.

It's a life that we live "by faith in the Son of God" – we do not attain it through our good deeds or merits. The *only* way we can achieve this new life is *by faith*.

His final sentence is the knock-out punch against his opponents: "I do not set aside the grace of God, for if righteousness could be gained through the law, Christ died for nothing!" Paul says that if we could have achieved righteousness through obeying the law, then Christ's death was all in vain. God might as well have written us a book that said, "Just try hard to keep the law", rather than sending us a Saviour. If we could be righteous just by trying hard, then Christ's death was unnecessary.

This is exactly why we need the grace of God – because we *cannot* achieve salvation by keeping the law. We do not have the power within us. Sin keeps us in chains; only the grace of God can break those chains in Jesus Christ.

As Charles Wesley put it in his famous hymn *And Can it Be:*

> Long my imprisoned spirit lay,
> Fast bound in sin and nature's night;
> Thine eye diffused a quick'ning ray –
> I woke, the dungeon flamed with light;
> My chains fell off, my heart was free,
> I rose, went forth, and followed Thee.

It was this wonderful teaching that the Reformation re-discovered. We do not achieve salvation through our own efforts, because such a thing would be impossible. Salvation can only be a gift of grace, through Jesus Christ.

Why was the law given at all? (3:23-25)

One question you might have is, if we can't be justified by obeying the law, then why was the law given in the first place? This is a good question, and one which Paul addresses here:

> Before the coming of this faith, we were held in custody under the law, locked up until the faith that was to come would be revealed. So the law was our guardian until Christ came that we might be justified by faith. Now that this faith has come, we are no longer under a guardian.
> *Galatians 3:23-25*

Paul describes the law as a "guardian". The word means someone who would look after children until they came of age. This is what the law was like: it looked after us, taught us how to live, until Christ came. The law was given to guide us while we did not have Christ and did not have the Holy Spirit. Paul says in another letter:

> We also know that the law is made not for the righteous but for lawbreakers and rebels, the ungodly and sinful, the unholy and irreligious.
> *1 Timothy 1:9*

The law was given originally to the Israelites to guide them in the right ways. They needed it because they didn't walk in those ways naturally. Because of disordered self-love, they needed some rules in black-and-white to show them what was loving and what wasn't. The law spelled it out for them in a way they could understand.

However, the law was never meant to be a way of achieving righteousness. In fact, it had the opposite effect – it exposed our own sinfulness and failure to love as God requires. The key point is,

61

righteousness *could not* come from the law – we do not have the power to obey within us. That can only come from the Holy Spirit.

Paul goes on to say, as a child has no need of a guardian when it reaches maturity, so also **we do not need the law now that Christ has come**. This may be a shocking thought, but Paul is totally sincere. We will return to this shortly.

Not patch-up but raise up!

Let's pause here for a moment. Paul is saying, as we saw in Chapter Three, that we are so sinful we need someone to come and save us. The problem extends far below the surface of our actions to our desires: we *do* the wrong things because we *want* the wrong things. Our desires are all wrong. The law might help us in a small way to control our behaviour, but it can never stop us *wanting* the wrong things. We need far more than a bit of help to get us across the line of obedience, but rather a death to our sinful selves and a whole new creation through Christ.

The renewal we need is the one we find in Christ – death followed by resurrection. When we believe in Jesus, we are united to him by faith. That means our sinful selves are nailed to the cross with Christ, where we die with him. But then, we are raised to new life with Christ and leave the empty tomb as a new creation. Christ does not put a few sticking plasters over our bad patches, but makes us completely new. As Paul says: "Therefore, if anyone is in Christ, the new creation has come: the old has gone, the new is here!" (2 Corinthians 5:17).

It doesn't just give us a bit of help sorting out our actions, it changes the things that we want *inside*. We can start to do the right things because we want the right things. We can start to act out of love for others rather than fear of breaking the law.

The important thing for our purposes here is that the resurrection life begins *right now*. We don't have to wait until the second coming! This is how the twentieth century pastor and theologian Francis Schaeffer summarised it:

> This is the basic consideration of the Christian life. First, Christ died in history. Second, Christ rose in history. Third, we died with Christ in history, when we accepted him as our Saviour. Fourth, we will be raised in history, when he comes again. Fifth, we are to live by faith now as though we were now dead, already have died. And sixth, we are to live now by faith as though we have now already been raised from the dead.[19]

What an astonishing statement: we are to live as though we have already been raised from the dead. Perhaps you have never thought of the Christian life this way before. And yet, that is exactly how Paul describes it! He says, "The death he died, he died to sin once for all; but the life he lives, he lives to God. In the same way, count yourselves dead to sin but alive to God in Christ Jesus" (Romans 6:10-11).

This accords with what Jesus says in John's Gospel: "Very truly I tell you, whoever hears my word and believes him who sent me has eternal life and will not be judged but has crossed over from death to life" (John 5:24). Crossing over from death to life is described by Jesus here – and consistently in John's Gospel – as a past event. When we believe in Jesus, we cross over from death to life. Our new life doesn't begin in the future, it begins *now*.

---

[19] Francis Schaeffer, *True Spirituality* (Hodder & Stoughton: 1973), 53

All this should raise a fundamental question. *How* do we begin to enjoy that life? If you're anything like me, most of the time our experience in this life does not seem very 'new creation'. We still feel the effects of sin in our own lives, let alone in the world. What we're going to do now is skip to the last couple of chapters of Galatians, where Paul deals specifically with the question of how we start to live that kind of life.

Freedom! (5:1)

> It is for freedom that Christ has set us free. Stand firm, then, and
> do not let yourselves be burdened again by a yoke of slavery. (5:1)

These are wonderful and inspiring words. It's the kind of verse you might put on a fridge magnet! But what does it really mean?

Paul is saying to the Galatians, given everything that he has said – *don't go back to the law*! The Christian life for them should no longer be about observing the law, the way the Jewish Christians had been teaching. Instead, Paul says that Christ has set us free: the Christian life is now about *freedom*. Whereas the law was a "yoke of slavery" – as we saw with the "guardian" from chapter three – we are now to live for freedom.

We often miss the importance of these words because we think that Paul simply *can't* mean the plain, black-and-white sense of what he says. But I believe he literally means that **we are now free from the law**.

In the parts of Galatians we skipped over, he was building up the case that the law was absolutely not how we were to be made righteous. But, more than that, our lives were to be lived "by faith" rather than "by the law" (see what he says in 3:11-12). The two things are mutually exclusive – you can either live by faith, or you can live by the law. It cannot be both.

At this point you might find yourself thinking: "Hold on, Paul. You *can't* be saying we're free. I mean, really, really free. Doesn't that mean we could do ... anything? Doesn't that mean we could sin with impunity?! We can't REALLY be free, surely?!!"

To answer that question, we need to look at one more passage.

Freedom is not freedom to sin (5:13-26)

This is not a short passage, but it's important to quote it in full as it's the climax of the argument we are making. It brings together everything we've seen so far. I'll try to break it down into manageable chunks.

> You, my brothers and sisters, were called to be free. But do not use your freedom to indulge the flesh; rather, serve one another humbly in love. For the entire law is fulfilled in keeping this one command: 'Love your neighbour as yourself.' If you bite and devour each other, watch out or you will be destroyed by each other. (5:13-15)

Paul starts out by repeating that we were called to be free. "But", he says, "do not use your freedom to indulge the flesh." The "flesh" is Paul's way of referring to our sinful nature. The NIV Bible helpfully footnotes: "the Greek word for *flesh* refers to the sinful state of human beings, often presented as a power in opposition to the Spirit". The "flesh" encompasses our wrong and sinful desires – disordered self-love, as we were thinking about in Chapter Three.

So, Paul says explicitly that freedom does not mean indulging our sinful desires. Instead, he says we should "serve one another humbly in love". The reason is, "the entire law is fulfilled in keeping this one command: 'Love your neighbour as yourself.'" So, our freedom is not to serve ourselves and our own sinful desires, but to serve each other in love. As we saw in Chapter One, he quotes the law of love and says that is the one command we need to obey.

He goes on to contrast love with "biting and devouring each other" – in other words, acting in a selfish and harmful way. This is the opposite of love, and will lead to destruction. Paul reminds us that *freedom* doesn't mean freedom from consequences. If we use our freedom to do wrong, we will face the consequences of our actions. He says later (v21) that those who wilfully continue in sin will not inherit the kingdom of God. We'll come onto that in a moment.

You might be thinking: "Well, that's all very well, Paul. But *how* do I go about living a life of love?" That's the exact question that Paul turns to.

> So I say, live by the Spirit, and you will not gratify the desires of the flesh. For the flesh desires what is contrary to the Spirit, and the Spirit what is contrary to the flesh. They are in conflict with each other, so that you are not to do whatever you want. But if you are led by the Spirit, you are not under the law.
>
> The acts of the flesh are obvious: sexual immorality, impurity and debauchery; idolatry and witchcraft; hatred, discord, jealousy, fits of rage, selfish ambition, dissensions, factions and envy; drunkenness, orgies, and the like. I warn you, as I did before, that those who live like this will not inherit the kingdom of God.
>
> But the fruit of the Spirit is love, joy, peace, forbearance, kindness, goodness, faithfulness, gentleness and self-control. Against such things there is no law. (5:16-23)

Paul outlines two contrasting ways of living: either by "the flesh", or by the Spirit. They are "in conflict with each other" – mutually exclusive –

"so that you are not to do whatever you want". He acknowledges the criticism that "freedom" could be seen as a license to indulge our sinful desires – but that couldn't be further from his message.

Instead, Paul says that it is only the spiritual life which will truly lead to holy living. He says, if you "live by the Spirit, you will not gratify the desires of the flesh". The Spirit living in us will keep us from simply indulging our own sinful desires. In fact, the Spirit will not only keep us from sinful self-indulgence but will bear good fruit in us. Paul spells out what the difference is between the "flesh" and the Spirit in vv19-23:

The acts of the flesh	The fruit of the Spirit
Sexual immorality	Love
Impurity	Joy
Debauchery	Peace
Idolatry	Forbearance
Witchcraft	Kindness
Hatred	Goodness
Discord	Faithfulness
Fits of rage	Gentleness
Selfish ambition	Self-control
Dissensions	
Factions	
Envy	
Drunkenness	
Orgies	

The acts of the flesh are, as Paul says, "obvious": they are self-centred acts which destroy relationships and communities. They do not show love for God or neighbour, instead they look like the disordered self-love we saw in Chapter Three. He goes on, "those who live like this will not inherit the kingdom of God." Again, we are told that there is a consequence for living selfish and ungodly lives. Those who live in this way prove themselves to be outside of the kingdom of God, and will experience punishment along with unbelievers.

Paul is fully aware of the criticism that freedom in Christ will lead to immoral living, but he vigorously rejects that claim. Those who simply use their freedom to live in sin show that they have not been saved from it. How can we carry on living in sin if we have been saved from sin? Such a thing would be an impossibility! This is exactly what we are told elsewhere in the New Testament:

> If we deliberately keep on sinning after we have received the knowledge of the truth, no sacrifice for sins is left, but only a fearful expectation of judgment and of raging fire that will consume the enemies of God.
> *Hebrews 10:26-27*

By contrast, those who truly belong to Christ, who are living by the Spirit, will grow in the fruit of the Spirit.

Notice that Paul uses the singular word, "fruit", rather than fruits. This is because the one fruit is *love* – everything else on the list is an outworking of love. This is the reason Paul can say: "Against such things there is no law." Those who live by the Spirit, who bear the fruit of the Spirit in their lives, are freed from the law: they *will* keep the law because they love. But the obedience does not come from themselves – it comes from God, through the Holy Spirit.

Paul finishes with a summary statement:

> Those who belong to Christ Jesus have crucified the flesh with its passions and desires. Since we live by the Spirit, let us keep in step with the Spirit. (5:24-26)

Paul starts by affirming that we have been crucified with Christ. It is done – it is a past event. We are, as we saw before, to consider ourselves "dead to sin" (Romans 6:11). It is another reminder that what we need is not a touch-up job on our old selves, but to put to death "the flesh" and rise to a new creation in Christ Jesus. We do that by living by the Spirit and keeping in step with him.

In the next chapter we will consider more practically what that looks like.

Chapter Five: How do we keep in step with the Spirit?

A bit more detail needed...?

In Chapter Four, we studied Paul's explanation of the Christian life in Galatians. However, one aspect of the letter which needs more explanation is what it means, practically speaking, to "walk in step with the Spirit". Perhaps, upon reading that, you thought: "Thanks for that, Paul, but I don't know how to put it into practice!" In this chapter, we are going to explore what it means to live in step with the Spirit in our day-to-day lives.[20]

Let's think about what the Christian life involves more generally. This is Jesus' summary of his teaching according to Mark's gospel:

> After John was put in prison, Jesus went into Galilee, proclaiming the good news of God. "The time has come," he said. "The kingdom of God has come near. Repent and believe the good news!"
> *Mark 1:14-15*

---

[20] J.I. Packer wrote a book *Keep in Step with the Spirit* on this topic, which I can thoroughly recommend.

The phrase Jesus chose to summarise his teaching is "repent and believe". These two ideas, *repentance* and *faith*, are a fundamental summary of what it means to follow Jesus.[21] These elements are the building blocks of the Christian life. We're going to take them in turn to see how we can make sense of Paul's instruction to walk in step with the Spirit.

#1: Repentance

What IS repentance?

If you've been around in church for a while, you are probably familiar with the word 'repentance'. As we've just seen, it is at the heart of the Christian faith. However, it may seem like an old-fashioned word, especially if you are new to Christianity. It's not a word which is used in everyday language! So, what does it mean?

The word 'repent' in our English Bibles is the translation of a Greek word *metanoia* which means "to change one's mind". The idea behind Biblical repentance is that we think wrongly, and so we need to change our thinking and bring it into line with God's.[22] You could liken it to soldiers doing an "about turn": we start out going in the wrong direction, and we end up going in the right direction.

Of course, repentance affects much more than our minds – it will change our actions as well. But it needs to start with our minds because that's where our actions begin. Our actions are the practical demonstration of what we believe. For example, if you believe eating meat is a bad thing, you won't eat meat. If you believe that fitness and exercise is good,

---

[21] Compare with Jesus' summary at the end of Luke's gospel - Luke 24:47
[22] Paul spells this out in Romans 12:2, "be transformed by the renewing of your mind".

you'll take up sports or running or the like. We act according to our beliefs.

This why repentance in the Bible may start with the mind, but it involves the whole person. It means to turn away from our evil ways and turn instead to God's ways of righteousness. We change our minds and therefore our actions to bring them in line with how God wants us to be.

Paul teaches us about repentance in another letter, 2 Corinthians. He had previously written to the church to rebuke them for their sinful ways, and they had listened to him and changed. This is how he responds to them:

> Even if I caused you sorrow by my letter, I do not regret it. Though I did regret it — I see that my letter hurt you, but only for a little while — yet now I am happy, not because you were made sorry, but because your sorrow led you to repentance. For you became sorrowful as God intended and so were not harmed in any way by us. Godly sorrow brings repentance that leads to salvation and leaves no regret, but worldly sorrow brings death. See what this godly sorrow has produced in you: what earnestness, what eagerness to clear yourselves, what indignation, what alarm, what longing, what concern, what readiness to see justice done.
> *2 Corinthians 7:8-11*

In this passage Paul contrasts "worldly sorrow" with "Godly sorrow". Worldly sorrow is simply regret for acting in a certain way. Paul says this "brings death" because it falls short of what God wants from us – it does not cause change. Godly sorrow, on the other hand, brings true repentance – it means that we *genuinely change our behaviour*. Their repentance was shown by the fact that they didn't just make a spectacle

72

of how sorry they were, they amended their lives. True repentance is more than regret; repentance always leads to a changed life.

We see this difference in the world all the time. I have two young children, and when they have done something naughty I will tell them off. Sometimes they say "sorry" – but then moments later continue doing the very thing I told them off for. I have to say to them: that is not sorry! If you are genuinely sorry, you will stop doing the thing which you were told off for in the first place. If we keep doing the wrong thing, we show that we're not really sorry. In the words of that well-known theologian, Rihanna:

> Don't tell me you're sorry 'cause you're not
> Baby, when I know you're only sorry you got caught.[23]

The Corinthians weren't only sorry they got caught. They had really listened to Paul's rebuke and were willing and eager to change. This is true repentance.

There is one more thing we need to understand about repentance: sometimes people have the idea that we only need to repent at the start of our Christian lives. In other words, we repent on the day we believe in Jesus, but then we don't need to think about it again. This could not be further from the truth.

Repentance is more like a lifestyle – something we need to do day-by-day. It should come as naturally to us as breathing. Martin Luther, who we have mentioned briefly already, kick started the Reformation on 31st October 1517 when he posted up his 95 Theses to the door of the church in Wittenberg. The very first one read:

---

[23] Rihanna, *Take a Bow*

> Our Lord and Master Jesus Christ, when He said "Repent", willed that the whole life of believers should be repentance.[24]

Luther understood that repentance was not a one-off confession at the start of our Christian lives, but was – in a sense – our whole lives. Repentance is simply how we should be towards God, every day, even every moment of every day. You could say it's simply our "posture" towards God – we should *always* be repentant.

This makes sense when you think about how sinful we are: it's not as if we only have to repent when we've done some specific sin. We *always* need to turn from our sinful and selfish ways to God's ways of love. That's how fundamental repentance is.

Turning from sin to righteousness

Having established what repentance is, we can now start to think about how it helps us with living by the Spirit. Let's start out by considering what we would think of repentance if we had a Pharisaical view of the law – as we saw in Chapter Two. Take the command: "Do not steal", for example.

If you only think of the commands on a surface level, then how do you think repentance would apply to this command? Presumably the Pharisees would have said it only applied to someone who had taken something without the owner's consent. If you stole something, then you would need to ask for God's forgiveness, be reconciled with the person you stole from (including returning or replacing what you stole!), and then promise not to steal again.

---

[24] See online: www.worldhistory.org/article/1891/martin-luthers-95-theses/

That's probably how we would teach the commands to children – you've done a bad thing, so you need to say sorry and stop doing the bad thing.

But think about it: this leaves out half of repentance, doesn't it? Repentance isn't simply about *stopping* doing something bad. It's about turning away from what's bad <u>AND ALSO</u> turning to what's good. If we see the commandments only in a wooden, black-and-white kind of way, we will reduce repentance simply to saying "sorry" in the way that children do. That is not Biblical repentance.

We need to see the commandments through this lens. Every command contains things which are forbidden, as well as things which we should be doing instead. Within each command there are things to turn from and to.

Let's go back to our example. What does "Do not steal" look like given the more complex, Biblical view of repentance? It is not simply about "stealing" but applies more broadly to how we love others and all they own. The Heidelberg Catechism[25] does a good job of showing in all the commandments what is forbidden, as well as what is required of us (i.e. what we should turn from and to). This is what it says of the Eighth Commandment:

> God forbids not only outright theft and robbery…
> we must not defraud our neighbour in any way,

---

[25] A Catechism is a way of teaching the Christian faith through a series of questions and answers. It was probably developed by the church in the early days to teach baptism candidates what the Christian faith was. The Heidelberg Catechism was published in 1563, at the time of the Reformation. It is one of the most well-known catechisms of the Protestant church and is still in print today.

whether by force or by show of right.
In addition God forbids all greed
    and all abuse or squandering of his gifts.

This is what we should repent of – not just theft and robbery, but fraud, greed, and abusing the gifts which he has given us. Clearly, this is a lot wider than simply "stealing" (in the way most of us think of it). But there's more. The catechism goes on with what we should turn to:

I must promote my neighbour's good
    wherever I can and may,
deal with him
    as I would like others to deal with me,
and work faithfully
    so that I may be able to give
    to those in need.[26]

The catechism rightly points out the command "Do not steal" requires that we actively promote our neighbour's good – even to the point of working to be able to give to those in need. It's a total change of attitude. Instead of stopping at what we should not do, it continues to the way that we should behave instead – in this case, by being generous. (We'll think more about this command in the next chapter).

Do you see how all this makes 'repentance' a much more significant concept? Repentance means carefully considering not just what we have done wrong, but *what we should have done instead*. It means actively turning from the wrong ways in which we have walked, to the right ways in which God wants us to walk – the path of love. We need to turn

---

[26] See online: http://www.heidelberg-catechism.com/en/lords-days/42.html

continually from the one to the other. However, without faith, repentance is of limited value – so let's turn now to think about faith.

#2: Faith

What is faith?

The second element of the Christian life we need to look at is *faith*. What is faith? The classic definition of faith in the Bible is found in the book of Hebrews:

> Now faith is confidence in what we hope for and assurance about what we do not see.
> *Hebrews 11:1*

So, faith is taking "what we hope for", i.e. the promises God has made to us in the Bible – and having confidence in them. Faith is not simply *knowing* what God has said to us but putting it into practice. It's the difference between merely knowing the statement "Jesus died on the cross for my sins" and repenting of our sins every day and trusting in Jesus for our salvation.

The important thing is, true faith leads to action. It's a bit like the difference we saw in the previous section between worldly sorrow and Godly sorrow.

Where does faith come from? People sometimes think about faith as being something that some people have and others don't. There's a scene in *The Matrix* where Morpheus tells Neo, "You have to let it all go, Neo – fear, doubt, and disbelief." Neo was

required to believe, it had to come from within him. And he wouldn't be able to do what he needed to do unless he reached a certain level of faith.

This is not what Biblical faith is like! Paul tells us:

> For it is by grace you have been saved, through faith – and this is not from yourselves, it is the gift of God
> *Ephesians 2:8*

Faith is "not from yourselves" – it is "the gift of God" (see also Romans 12:3). Faith is not something which some people have naturally and others don't. We don't have to work our way up to faith in our own strength like Neo. Rather, faith is something which is given from God, through the power of the Holy Spirit (1 Corinthians 12:9).

Let's summarise what we've learned so far. Faith is:

(1) Not simply *knowing* God's promises but *trusting* in them so that it changes the way that we live.
(2) A gift of God through the Holy Spirit.

Let's think through how this helps us to repent.

How do we know what to repent of?
After reading the section on repentance, you might have wondered: "How do I know what to repent of, and how to live?" It's not always easy to know the right course of action, especially in the messy world we live in. If you interpret the commands in a wooden way, then repenting of theft is a straightforward matter. But, as we saw, if you think about *love* being behind the commands then it's not so easy! It means we need to treat individuals and situations with care and wisdom.

This is where faith comes in. Psalm 1 begins like this:

> Blessed is the one
>   who does not walk in step with the wicked
> or stand in the way that sinners take
>   or sit in the company of mockers,
> but whose delight is in the law of the Lord,
>   and who meditates on his law day and night.
> *Psalm 1:1-2*

This psalm says that the opposite of doing evil is to take "delight" in the law of the Lord. How do we take delight in God's law? By meditating on his law "day and night" – in other words, all the time.

The word *meditating* is key to unlocking God's law. Many Christians are hesitant about meditation because it has connotations of Eastern religions and secular 'spirituality'. In those cases, it usually involves emptying your mind and focussing on your breathing, or senses, and so on. But Biblical, Christian meditation is not like that at all. Christian meditation involves filling our mind with God's Word. It involves turning over God's Word and what it means for us in our minds.

That might seem like a hard task: how do we know that we're meditating rightly on the Bible? How do we know we're taking the right things from it? Fortunately, there is some very good news: we are not on our own, but we have the help of the Holy Spirit! The Spirit inspired Scripture (2 Timothy 3:16), and the same Spirit lives in us and helps us to understand the Scriptures today. It's a bit like reading a book while you have the author sitting with you, who can explain all the parts you don't understand.

When we come to the Bible to meditate on God's Word (the whole Bible, not just the commandments), seeking to hear from him, then he will speak to us. The Spirit can make God's Word come alive to us and illuminate our present circumstances. God's Word is powerful and speaks to us today.

My experience is, if I am struggling for wisdom in knowing how to love someone, I often don't need to look any further than my daily Bible reading. I try to read the Bible every day, and I find that the words I read will often speak to me about a particular situation I am facing, usually in a surprising and mysterious way! When we read the Scriptures in the hope and expectation that God will speak to us, we shouldn't be surprised when he does speak. He will lead us to how we can please him and love others.

At the end of the day, it comes down to how well we know the Bible. The better we know the Bible, the more we will know how God wants us to apply his commands in any given situation. Spend time meditating on the Bible, asking him for his insight, and he will give it. James 1:5 says, "If any of you lacks wisdom, you should ask God, who gives generously to all without finding fault, and it will be given to you". This neatly brings us to the final section.

The foundational importance of prayer

We've thought about learning to love other people by meditating on God's Word. The question we now turn to is, how do we put that knowledge into practice? The problem of sin is that we *don't* love other people. Knowing how we should love them is a part of the battle, but the far greater challenge is the ability to do it. This is where we need the transforming power of the Holy Spirit in our lives. But how do we access that power?

The Reformation theologian John Calvin once called prayer, "the chief exercise of faith". What he meant by that is, our faith is shown by the way that we depend upon God in prayer. This is very different to how Christians sometimes talk about prayer. We often say that it is something Christians just need to do, some kind of chore like mopping the floor or making your bed. Can you imagine if we treated talking to our spouse in that way? "I'm talking to you because it's something I have to do"!

On the contrary, prayer is an expression of our relationship with God. In prayer we depend on him, bring our needs to him, ask for his help, and entrust ourselves to him. In many ways, prayer is the most important thing that we need to be doing – it underpins everything else.

In prayer we come to God in repentance for our sins ("forgive us our sins as we forgive"), and ask for our daily needs ("give us our daily bread"). In prayer we ask for guidance ("lead us not into temptation"). Prayer is, in a sense, the engine room of the Christian life: it powers everything else. I hope that this helps you to see how prayer is related to everything we've discovered about repentance. In prayer we come to God for forgiveness, and we ask him for his strength to do what he asks of us. In prayer we ask for the Holy Spirit to bear his fruit in our lives.

In short, when we pray, we take all our sinfulness to God, ask him to forgive us, and give us the love that we need.

Prayer turns repentance from being an abstract concept into something concrete which we experience. This is why we need to be committed to prayer. The apostle Paul says, "pray in the Spirit on all occasions with all kinds of prayers and requests" (Ephesians 6:18). Or, more concisely, "pray continually" (1 Thessalonians 5:17). Prayer, like repentance, should be as natural to us as breathing. When we pray, we come to God as penitent sinners, asking for his help in our needs.

In prayer we recognise our *dependence* on God in every way. Sometimes we might need to ask for forgiveness for specific sins. But all the time we need to ask for God's help. When I pray, the word 'help' is my most-used word! It's never far from my mind. We also need to thank God for the gifts he's given us and the help he has provided so far, trusting that he will do so again.

We saw earlier that as we read God's Word, in the power of the Holy Spirit, we discern our faults and our needs. It is only as we pray that we receive power to change our lives in accordance with God's will. It puts God's power behind repentance. The great theologian Augustine once said: "Give what You command, and command what You will"[27]. In other words, we can only fulfil God's commands by God's power working in us. Prayer is the only way for us to access God's power.

Putting it together

Let's finish this chapter by pulling together what we've learned. This is the best way I have come up with to summarise how the Christian life works. It's a 'virtuous cycle' (the opposite of a vicious cycle).

---

[27] See online: https://www.newadvent.org/fathers/110110.htm (Chapter 29)

1. **Reading the Word** – as we read and meditate on the Scriptures, we recognise how far short we fall of God's ways.
2. **Repentance** – we turn to God in prayer, asking him for his forgiveness for our lack of love and the help we need to love him and others.
3. **Grace** – we find his grace as we receive his forgiveness through Jesus Christ and the fruit of the Holy Spirit in our lives.
4. **Gratitude** – finding his grace inspires us to live with gratitude and love for him and gives us confidence to keep going back to his Word again.

Of course, the Holy Spirit is involved at every stage of the process: the Spirit helps us to understand the word, to know our own sinfulness, to pray, to know Jesus' grace in our lives, and to live out gratitude. It is through the Spirit that these things are more than words but become real in our lives.

Chapter Six: A fresh look at the Ten Commandments

The Commandments of love

Over the course of this book, we have been thinking about how God's laws of love stand behind all the commandments. In particular, the Ten Commandments were designed to teach us how to love. They were addressed to sinners, and so put in negative terms, but were intended to show us practically what love looked like.

We are going to finish this book by working through the Ten Commandments to see how each of them find their fulfilment in loving God and our neighbour. This is the longest chapter in the book, but there's much more you could say (you could easily write a book on the Ten Commandments alone – and maybe I will one day!). If you would like to study the Ten Commandments as a series, and go into a little more detail, you might be interested in the Understand the Bible video series on the Ten Commandments.[28]

---

[28] Available online: https://understandthebible.uk/courses/the-ten-commandments/

Although this chapter cannot be comprehensive, my hope is that it will cause you to think and reflect for yourself, especially as you are considering how these commandments apply to the circumstances of your own life. I would suggest prayerfully working your way through the commandments and asking God to help you understand if there are any changes that he wants you to make. If you ask him, he will help you to know where you need his power to change and what to be aiming for.

Following on from our discussion of repentance in Chapter Five, in this chapter we are going to look at the 'positive' and 'negative' aspects of each commandment. In other words, what we should turn *from* (negative), and what we should turn *to* (positive). I hope that looking at each commandment in turn will give you some ideas as to how we can repent and grow in love.

How the commandments are structured

Before we start looking at the commandments themselves, let's think for a moment about how they are structured. The commandments were given on two tablets of stone (Exodus 31:18). This has caused theologians through the years to see the commandments as being divided into two parts – corresponding to the first and second greatest commands (love for God and neighbour).

There has been some disagreement as to exactly where the line should be drawn – as we will see, it's not a black-and-white issue. However, I would say that the first four commandments are *generally* oriented towards love for God, whereas the rest are oriented more towards love for neighbour. This is how we will consider the commandments in this chapter. Of course, it doesn't really make a difference to our obedience, but it might be helpful for you to think of it in these terms.

Another important thing to note before we get onto the commandments themselves is that they begin with a reminder of God's salvation:

> I am the Lord your God, who brought you out of Egypt, out of the land of slavery.
> *Exodus 20:2*

God rescued his people *before* he gave them the law. This is a picture of grace: He didn't ask them to obey to make themselves acceptable to him. He asked them to obey out of love for him, for what he had already done for them. It's the same for us as Christians: God saves us first, and then calls us to a holy life. As Paul says: "He has saved us and called us to a holy life – not because of anything we have done but because of his own purpose and grace" (2 Timothy 1:9).

We must always remember that we do not earn God's salvation – it is a free gift of God's grace. We also know that the power to obey God's commands does not come from ourselves – it comes from the Holy Spirit. It's vitally important to understand that this is not about earning God's salvation or simply "trying harder". What we read here is helping us to understand where we need to repent and ask for God's help.

#1: You shall have no other gods before me

In the first command, the Lord says that he should be our Number One. We must have no other gods before him – he alone should be the Lord of our lives. I hope it is straightforward to see how this commandment expresses what it means to love the Lord with our heart, soul, mind, and strength: we should love him enough to make him our first priority.

This command says that we should not put other gods above God. The first question we need to deal with is – does that mean there is more than one God? The short answer is, "no"! Elsewhere, God makes clear that he is the only God (e.g. Deuteronomy 6:4, which is also quoted by Jesus).

So, if there are no other gods, how can we put them above him? To understand this properly, we need to understand that some things which are not God are "gods" in our lives. The Bible calls these *idols*. An idol doesn't have to be a physical object in the shape of a god, such as a statue of Baal. On the contrary, it could be a physical thing such as money or possessions, or even something intangible such as fame, success, or happiness. It is anything which operates as a kind of God-substitute in our lives – and we could have several of them.

What is the problem with idols and idolatry – the worship of idols? In the Old Testament book of Jeremiah we read these words:

> Has a nation ever changed its gods?
>   (Yet they are not gods at all.)
> But my people have exchanged their glorious God
>   for worthless idols.
> Be appalled at this, you heavens,
>   and shudder with great horror,"
> declares the Lord.
> "My people have committed two sins:
> They have forsaken me,
>   the spring of living water,
> and have dug their own cisterns,
>   broken cisterns that cannot hold water.
> *Jeremiah 2:11-13*

Here the Old Testament people of Israel are accused of exchanging their glorious God for worthless idols. Yet these idols were not gods at all! This is the tragedy of idolatry – we substitute our glorious God for poor imitations, things which will never satisfy. Our God alone is the fountain of living water – false gods are like broken cisterns which cannot hold water. If we seek from them what only God can provide, we will never be happy. We need to repent of the times we trust in things other than the Lord to do what only he can do for us.

So, what does obedience to this command look like?

Firstly, we should dedicate ourselves to **knowing God**. Jesus said: "Now this is eternal life: that they know you, the only true God, and Jesus Christ, whom you have sent" (John 17:3). According to Jesus, eternal life is about *knowing* God. Loving someone and knowing someone go together – so it is with God. Therefore we can fulfil this command by dedicating ourselves to knowing God better.

If I only ever speak to my wife about managing the practicalities of our lives, and never because I simply enjoy her company, do you think that would be a good and healthy relationship? I think it would rather be a sign of an unhealthy relationship! It's like that with God. We should seek to know him, to be with him, to listen to him, day by day. That means dedicating ourselves to reading and understanding his Word (the Bible) and taking time to pray to him often.

It also means being *honest* with God – honest about the way we feel and what we want. I always used to pray in a way that I thought God wanted me to pray – trying to hide the worst bits of myself and my desires. It took me many years before I finally allowed myself to be truly honest with God in prayer. I eventually thought, "God knows what I'm really like anyway, so I might as well be open with him." This has helped hugely in getting to know God better. It's far better to take your struggles, your desires, your fears, and so on to God with complete honesty and leave them in his hands. Your intimacy with God will grow.

Secondly, we should **submit to God** in everything. Peter says: "Humble yourselves, therefore, under God's mighty hand, that he may lift you up in due time" (1 Peter 5:6). If we love the Lord, we should obey him in humility and trust that he will lead us and give us the things we need to obey him. *Even if* that means coming into conflict with the way the world does things; if God says it, we should obey it – regardless of what people say. We should love God enough to obey him, even if obedience is costly. Many Christians through history have loved God enough to lose their lives for him: "they did not love their lives so much as to shrink from death" (Revelation 12:11). They had the strength to be martyrs for Christ because they loved him even more than their own lives.

However, we must understand that to humble ourselves before God is a good thing. We mustn't be resentful of God – in fact, quite the opposite:

> Take delight in the Lord,
>   and he will give you the desires of your heart.
> *Psalm 37:4*

As we come to know God better, as we honestly open our hopes and fears up to him, we will begin to understand how he is able to fulfil us in a deeper way than we can imagine. Loving God may be hard sometimes, but it is also the best thing in the world!

Thirdly, we should **honour God in all that we do**. As Paul says: "Whatever you do, work at it with all your heart, as working for the Lord, not for human masters" (Colossians 3:23). This means that we should seek God's help and his will in *everything* we do. God wants us to seek him in every part of our lives – everything we do to work and play, not just our 'spiritual' activities.

A theologian of the early church called Irenaeus once said: "The glory of God is man fully alive". As we love God and seek his will and help in everything we do, we become more alive – we grow into the people God wants us to be. As we start to love God truly, we start to become our true selves.

#2: You shall not make idols

This command is much longer than the first:

> "You shall not make for yourself an image in the form of anything
> in heaven above or on the earth beneath or in the waters
> below. You shall not bow down to them or worship them; for I,
> the Lord your God, am a jealous God, punishing the children for
> the sin of the parents to the third and fourth generation of those
> who hate me, but showing love to a thousand generations of
> those who love me and keep my commandments.
> *Exodus 20:4-6*

This command forbids the making of "images", or what we more commonly call idols. It goes without saying that twenty-first century Westerners are probably not going to fashion a golden calf and bow down to it, as the ancient Israelites did. Not explicitly, anyway – as we've already seen, lots of things can function as God-substitutes, even if they do not look like gods. But the point remains that today, few people are tempted to make gods in the way they did in the ancient world. We do not have household gods or a household shrine anymore. So how is this command relevant to us?

Although we may not have 'gods' in the same way as the ancient world did, we do still treat some things as if they had supernatural powers. For example, good luck charms are common today. People think that some things are 'lucky' and will bring you good fortune, whereas other things are 'unlucky'. This is effectively a form of idolatry – believing something in creation has supernatural power. Some people have little Buddha statues or figurines in their window – do they have them because they think they are keeping evil spirits away? In which case, again, this is a violation of the command.

The second command means that we should not treat any created thing as if it were a god. God is bigger than heaven and earth, he cannot be reduced to something in the universe. If you want any good thing – protection from evil, success, and so on – then you need to ask God, not a figurine or a good luck charm.

We can also violate this command by *imagining* what God is like, rather than looking to the Bible to see what he has to say about himself. We should not think that God will conform to our expectations of him; rather, we should seek to conform to his expectations of us. As C.S. Lewis says of Aslan in *The Lion, The Witch and the Wardrobe*, "he is not a tame lion" – he does not bow to our expectations.

Allow me to illustrate using *Star Trek: The Next Generation*. In one episode, the engineer Geordi La Forge creates a holographic representation of his engineering hero, Dr Leah Brahms. The computer generates it based on her personal records and published works, so it  looks and talks like the real thing. Despite knowing the hologram is only a fake, Geordi starts to fall in love. However, in a subsequent episode, La Forge meets the real Brahms and discovers that she is quite different. She is angry with him and feels that he has violated her by creating an inaccurate holographic representation of her.

Geordi believed that he was in love with Leah Brahms – but he was only in love with a computer-generated fiction which looked like the real thing. In the same way, it's possible for us to think that we love the Lord, but in reality we are loving a god of our own imagination.

Love and truth must go together: if we want to love God with our heart, soul, mind and strength, then we need to know him *truly*. And, of course, to know God truly means to know his Son, Jesus Christ: "No one has ever seen God, but the one and only Son, who is himself God and is in closest relationship with the Father, has made him known" (John 1:18). We need to repent of all the ways we relate to God other than through Jesus.

So, what does it mean to keep this command? Look back to what the Lord says: "I, the Lord your God, am a jealous God, punishing the children for the sin of the parents ... but showing love to a thousand generations of those who love me." God is a God of justice, as well as a God of love. To keep this command, we must look at Jesus – the one who perfectly satisfied God's justice by becoming an atoning sacrifice for us, the one who took the punishment for sin upon himself so that we might be forgiven.

For us to love God truly, we need to come through Jesus Christ. As he said: "No one comes to the Father except through me" (John 14:6). Jesus brings us to the Father, in the power of the Holy Spirit. Worshipping God truly means worshipping Father, Son and Holy Spirit. As we come to know Jesus, he brings us into a relationship with the Father and Spirit. The apostle John put it like this: "We proclaim to you what we have seen and heard, so that you also may have fellowship with us. And our fellowship is with the Father and with his Son, Jesus Christ" (1 John 1:3).

The positive side of not making an image of God is to truly enjoy "fellowship" – a close relationship – with God as he really is: Father, Son and Spirit. This is why the Trinity is such an important doctrine. It is not irrelevant to the Christian life, but it is how we experience God in our lives.[29] The antidote to making images of God is to know and experience God through Jesus Christ.

#3: You shall not misuse the name of the Lord

> You shall not misuse the name of the Lord your God, for
> the Lord will not hold anyone guiltless who misuses his name.
> *Exodus 20:7*

As a child, I was taught that this command meant we shouldn't use the names "God" or "Jesus" carelessly, like swear words. This is good advice for children, but the commandment goes much deeper than that. Modern people misunderstand this command because, to us, a "name" is simply a label. In the Bible, a name is much more than that.

In the world of the Bible, a "name" usually encompasses someone's whole reputation. For example, it says in Proverbs 22:1, "A good name is more desirable than great riches; to be esteemed is better than silver or gold." We still use the word in this way occasionally – for example, if

---

[29] For a good book to explain why the Trinity is so important, check out *The Good God* by Michael Reeves or *Delighting in the Trinity* by Tim Chester. Both of these are short and accessible. *Knowing God* by J.I. Packer is also a deservedly classic book.

someone has been found not guilty in a court case, we might say they "cleared their name".

The Bible makes clear that God is deeply concerned about his name. Think of one of the most famous passages in the Bible – Psalm 23:

> He guides me along the right paths
> **for his name's sake.**
> *Psalm 23:3*

Maybe you've read that Psalm hundreds of times yet never noticed that line! God is concerned for his name to be honoured among the nations, and especially among his people – the church. With that in mind, what does it mean to misuse God's name?

How we live as Christians impacts upon God's name or his reputation. This is what Paul says:

> You who boast in the law, do you dishonour God by breaking the law? As it is written: 'God's name is blasphemed among the Gentiles because of you.'
> *Romans 2:23-24*

One of the things which people find most off-putting about the church is hypocrisy. If people in the church proclaim a message of love on the one hand but live very selfish lives on the other, it reflects badly on God and Christianity. As Paul says, to live a hypocritical life like this is to dishonour God, and even to cause his name to be "blasphemed".

We must demonstrate our love for God by living lives of service to him, just as we saw in the first two commandments. In fact, keeping God's name is about living *authentic* Christian lives. It's not about being perfect – no-one is – but being forgiven and brought into a relationship with the Son of God, as we are transformed by the Holy Spirit day by day.

Jesus said, "If you love me, keep my commands" (John 14:15). As we love God and seek to keep his commands, we will demonstrate that his name is good. This also means that we will not promote our own name. The good that we do does not come from ourselves but by faith in Christ Jesus:

> I have been crucified with Christ and I no longer live, but Christ lives in me. The life I now live in the body, I live by faith in the Son of God, who loved me and gave himself for me.
> *Galatians 2:20*

As we live a life of love in the power of the Holy Spirit, and as we proclaim Christ by what we say and do, then we honour God's name. We also promote God's name to a watching world by living in his ways. People may deny the Bible, but they cannot deny the good that is accomplished in God's name or the love they experience.

Another aspect of honouring God's name for us as Christians is to remember the name of Jesus. He said:

> And I will do whatever you ask in my name, so that the Father may be glorified in the Son. You may ask me for anything in my name, and I will do it.
> *John 14:13-14*

Being concerned for the name of God also means being concerned for the name of Jesus. The two things go together. In this passage, Jesus says that we need to be concerned for his name – his reputation in the world. And if we pray and ask according to that, rather than for ourselves and our own name, he will answer prayer. It doesn't matter how big it is, all that matters is whose honour we are concerned with. That's a big promise – but this is not a book about prayer, so let's move on!

Pause to take stock...

Let's take a moment to pause and look back over where we've got to so far. The first three commands go together and form a kind of unit:

1. We honour God above everything else.
2. We honour him as he truly is.
3. We honour him with our lives.

You could summarise the first three commandments by saying we are commanded to enjoy a natural, authentic relationship with the God who made us, just like Adam and Eve did in the Garden of Eden (Genesis 3:8). As the Westminster Shorter Catechism famously puts it, our purpose is "to glorify God and enjoy him forever". This, in a nutshell, is what the first three commandments are about.

#4: Keep the Sabbath day holy

The first three commands focussed us on how we are to relate to God. In this fourth command, we start turning to more practical, everyday matters. This command marks the turning point where the focus shifts to our relationship with other people – although this command is really a transition because it has elements of both.

Before we get going, I need to add a little disclaimer. Sometimes I think the reason God gave us this command is to make it awkward for people doing a series on the Ten Commandments thousands of years later! The Sabbath command has – sadly – been a cause of contention and division among Christians. Some people advocate a strict observance of Sabbath – whether that be a Saturday or a Sunday. They say, "The command about murder is not abrogated – why should the Sabbath day be any different?" Other people claim that you don't have to keep any day special and would cite scriptures such as Romans 14:5-8 in support.

Some people have very strong feelings about this issue. A few years ago, our church received a letter which said that we were wrong and unbiblical to hold church services on a Sunday. Instead, we should have church services on a Saturday (as the fourth commandment says). In fact, it said that meeting on a Sunday was sinning against the Lord! So, it is with a sense of trepidation that I embark upon this territory. However, as we have seen, the commandments all have something important to say to us as Christians today, and it is therefore important to consider them all.

As we have seen through the course of this book, the commandments are an expression of God's intentions for us to love him and love others. This command, as with all the rest of them, can only be interpreted properly when we see it through this lens. Let's look at what it says:

> Remember the Sabbath day by keeping it holy. Six days you shall labour and do all your work, but the seventh day is a sabbath to the Lord your God. On it you shall not do any work, neither you, nor your son or daughter, nor your male or female servant, nor your animals, nor any foreigner residing in your towns. For in six days the Lord made the heavens and the earth, the sea, and all that is in them, but he rested on the seventh day. Therefore the Lord blessed the Sabbath day and made it holy.
> *Exodus 20:8-11*

The first thing we need to recognise is that this command is all about time and how we use it. Douglas Adams once said: "Time is an illusion. Lunchtime doubly so." That may be true – but illusion or no, we all have the same amount of it. We recognise the importance of using it wisely, as the sheer number of books about time management and productivity testify. We are told that if we want to achieve things, we must plan our time accordingly. Our usage of time reflects our goals and priorities.

This is significant, because how we use it says a lot about our priorities. For example, if I spent a large part of my time each week on football – watching it on TV, reading about it in the papers, going to see the game at weekends – you'd say that I loved football. Maybe even that that was the most important thing in my life. Alternatively, if I spent all my time at work – and none with my wife and children – you might say I loved my work more than them.

Is it therefore any surprise that God asks his people to keep a seventh of their week "holy" to him? God wanted his people to show their love and devotion to him by resting on the seventh day of the week. In other words, the fourth command was a practical demonstration that the people were living in obedience to the first three.

Note that the command was for them to "rest" – they were not to do any work on that day. (Nor were their servants – more on that in a moment). Does being commanded to "rest" one day in a week strike you as being harsh and unkind? Or the opposite?

Once again, the Pharisees help us to understand how it's possible to get this commandment wrong. On several occasions they came into conflict with Jesus about the specifics of the Sabbath. For example:

> One Sabbath Jesus was going through the grainfields, and as his disciples walked along, they began to pick some heads of grain. The Pharisees said to him, "Look, why are they doing what is unlawful on the Sabbath?"

> He answered, "Have you never read what David did when he and his companions were hungry and in need? In the days of Abiathar the high priest, he entered the house of God and ate the consecrated bread, which is lawful only for priests to eat. And he also gave some to his companions."

Then he said to them, "The Sabbath was made for man, not man for the Sabbath. So the Son of Man is Lord even of the Sabbath." *Mark 2:23-28*

The Pharisees had made the Sabbath into a chore – as with every other commandment. They turned it into a list of rules about what was and was not permissible on the Sabbath. But Jesus said, "The Sabbath was made for man, not man for the Sabbath" – in other words, it was *for our benefit*.

God intended for us to spend some time per week not working, but simply resting and enjoying him – because he knew that was good for us! In fact, as we are told in the commandment, the seven-day pattern is built into the very fabric of creation (see Genesis 2:3). It should come as no surprise that several people have tried changing the seven-day pattern without success.[30]

We were never designed to be workaholics – God wants us to take time to *enjoy* life. And it's not just about ourselves alone – taking time out from work is something that benefits the people around us. Think about it: if you work seven days a week, when do you get to spend time with your family or friends? When do you get to enjoy fellowship with other people, e.g. church? This is where the command starts to touch on love for others.

Let's take an example – opening shops on a Sunday. If you are a business owner and decide to open your shop on a Sunday, you will probably need to be there yourself, and you will need to have staff working too. If, on the other hand, you close your shop on a Sunday, you won't need

---

[30] See here for a recent example of someone trying a seven-day work week, and finding it didn't work out: buffer.com/resources/7-day-work-week-experiment-wisdom-day-rest/

to be there – and neither will your staff. So, closing on a Sunday means a day of rest not only for you, but also for your employees. In fact, a whole society that rests on one day a week is conducive to a healthy community. It gives time to rest and simply be with other people. (Those of us old enough to remember the days before the Sunday trading laws changed might like to reflect on whether seven-day shopping has been a good thing for our society.)

Therefore, it's important to think carefully about how we use our time. Time management is not simply a matter of efficiency but reflects our love for God and those around us. We should choose to use the limited time that we have well and wisely. As Paul says in Ephesians:

> Look carefully then how you walk, not as unwise but as
> wise, making the best use of the time, because the days are evil.
> *Ephesians 5:16-17 (ESV)*

God wants us to make the best use of our time, '24/7'. We are to use all day, every day, for him. He doesn't simply want a seventh of our week – he wants *all* of it. Every day we are to love him and love our neighbour. How we use our time matters deeply in how we express our priorities – so let's ask for his wisdom in using the time he has given us well.

Sidebar: a 'Sabbath rest'

One of the complicating factors in understanding the Sabbath is the way it is picked up by the author of Hebrews. Hebrews 4 takes the idea of sabbath rest and says it is representative of our eternal rest. He says:

> There remains, then, a Sabbath-rest for the people of God; for
> anyone who enters God's rest also rests from their works, just as
> God did from his.
> *Hebrews 4:9-10*

The idea is that 'resting' is more than a physical rest – it's really about resting from our "works". This means Sabbath is about trusting solely in Jesus for our salvation, and not trusting in our good works (as we looked at earlier in this book). If the Sabbath command was to teach God's Old Testament people the importance of spiritual 'rest', then as Christian believers it means that we should be living all our lives as 'rest' in that sense. Therefore, you could say that, for Christians, every day is a Sabbath day! We are to rest from our labours all the time.

We don't have time to delve into this area in more detail – although I would love to! – but do have a read of Hebrews and keep thinking and exploring.

#5: Honour your parents

The previous command was a transition – it had elements of loving God and loving our neighbour. From this command onwards, we are focussed unambiguously on loving our neighbour (until we get to the tenth command – but we will come onto that!).

> Honour your father and your mother, so that you may live long
> in the land the Lord your God is giving you.
> *Exodus 20:12*

It's significant that the word used is "honour" and not obey: honouring your parents might entail obeying them, especially for children, but honour is an expression of relationship. It means that we should honour them for as long as they live – which will look different when you're ten, twenty, or sixty. We honour our parents by loving them and doing what is best for them at all stages. For young children, that means obedience and submission. As adults, that means treating them with respect, love and kindness – such as seeking to look after them as they age.

However, this command has implications which are wider than the parent-child relationship. This is how the Heidelberg Catechism describes what the command requires of us:

That I show all honour, love, and faithfulness
    to my father and mother
    and to all those in authority over me,
submit myself with due obedience
    to their good instruction and discipline,
and also have patience with their weaknesses
    and shortcomings,
since it is God's will
    to govern us by their hand.[31]

The Catechism here expands "honour your parents" to include all authorities over us. God has given ways of governing the world, including the civil authorities (Romans 13:1-7) and employers (Ephesians 6:5-9)[32]. Therefore, love requires us to submit to appropriate authority and obey.

It is important to stress that this does not mean a blind obedience. Submission to authority is a teaching which has been misused by many tyrants and abusers through the years. There are many examples in the Bible of godly disobedience to authorities, such as Daniel in the Old Testament or the apostles in the New. The apostles said: "We must obey

---

[31] See online: http://www.heidelberg-catechism.com/en/lords-days/39.html
[32] This passage speaks of "slaves" and "masters", which is difficult for twenty-first century people to read without thinking of the transatlantic slave trade. However, things were very different in the first century. The closest parallel to today is probably that of an employee and an employer – however I do not have time to argue the case here!

God rather than human beings!" (Acts 5:29). So, obedience is not an absolute requirement – our duties to God come first.

It is also important to say that those in authority have responsibilities themselves. If any group or individual misuses authority, it should be dealt with appropriately. For example, submission to authority does not mean staying in an abusive relationship. Allowing an abuser to continue their abuse is not right. We should love people enough to challenge them when their behaviour needs to be challenged.

Finally, we must remember that Jesus transformed our understanding of family in the New Testament:

> Then Jesus' mother and brothers arrived. Standing outside, they sent someone in to call him. A crowd was sitting around him, and they told him, "Your mother and brothers are outside looking for you."
>
> "Who are my mother and my brothers?" he asked.
>
> Then he looked at those seated in a circle around him and said, "Here are my mother and my brothers! Whoever does God's will is my brother and sister and mother."
> *Mark 3:31-35*

Jesus says that his family is all those who do God's will. In other words, when we come to Jesus in repentance and faith, we become part of God's family. That doesn't make our biological families irrelevant, but it does relativise how important they are. I know several people who do not have good relationships with their biological family. For them, the church family *is* their family – **and that is exactly as it should be.**

This means that as a church we have duties to one another as Christians. For example, if someone is in need in your church, and you are able to help them, then you should. Paul says: "Therefore, as we have opportunity, let us do good to all people, especially to those who belong to the family of believers" (Galatians 6:10). It should be far more normal than it is to spend time with our fellow Christians and make a priority of simply being with them.

It struck me recently that we often talk about the church as being '*like* a family'. I think this is the wrong way round: the biological family is actually a picture of the church. The church is the real thing, the (biological) family is the shadow.

#6: You shall not murder

We come now to the command which everyone knows. If you asked people on the street to name the Ten Commandments, I expect most people would start with this one. This is probably because most people see how terrible murder is from the security of knowing that they themselves are not murderers. Like the Pharisees, everyone thinks they are keepers of this command *par excellence*. So much so that people think keeping this command is what makes them a good person. Several people have said to me: "I'm a good person – I've never murdered anyone".

If that was all there was to it, this would be a very short section, wouldn't it? "Don't murder anyone" – let's move on. But, as we have seen all the way through, it's not quite so simple. Think about it: if I beat someone to within an inch of their life and leave them on the floor naked and bleeding but still breathing – have I kept this command? What I have done is not technically 'murder', but surely my actions have been deeply immoral!

Once again, this is where we need to see the love behind the commandments. Jesus teaches on this command in the Sermon on the Mount:

> 'You have heard that it was said to the people long ago, "You shall not murder, and anyone who murders will be subject to judgment." But I tell you that anyone who is angry with a brother or sister will be subject to judgment. Again, anyone who says to a brother or sister, "Raca," is answerable to the court. And anyone who says, "You fool!" will be in danger of the fire of hell.

> 'Therefore, if you are offering your gift at the altar and there remember that your brother or sister has something against you, leave your gift there in front of the altar. First go and be reconciled to them; then come and offer your gift.

> 'Settle matters quickly with your adversary who is taking you to court. Do it while you are still together on the way, or your adversary may hand you over to the judge, and the judge may hand you over to the officer, and you may be thrown into prison. Truly I tell you, you will not get out until you have paid the last penny.
> *Matthew 5:21-26*

Jesus says that anyone who is angry with their brother or sister, or uses derogatory and insulting language toward them, is guilty of breaking the sixth commandment. This doesn't mean that those things are morally equivalent to murder. Rather, he means that those things are *covered by the same law*. The command not to murder anyone implies therefore that we shouldn't harm them in any way.

Jesus goes on to say this command means we should not stop at the avoidance of harm, but we should take the first step in reconciliation. If someone has something against us, we should be the one to make the first move in making things right. Jesus said we should even put it above "offering a gift at the altar" – showing how important it was.

If you haven't actually taken someone's life, it's easy to think this commandment is irrelevant to us. But which of us can say that we've never felt angry at our neighbour without just cause, or never wanted revenge? Which of us can say that we have always worked for our neighbour's good, even if they have treated us badly?

This command is a high calling to love our neighbour, even those who do not treat us well. We should never try to harm them, but always seek their good instead. This doesn't mean a 'one size fits all' approach – e.g., the best thing for criminals is to be punished appropriately and helped to amend their ways. Love needs to be tough sometimes – especially when it's about what is best for someone. As Proverbs 13:24 says, "Whoever spares the rod hates their children, but the one who loves their children is careful to discipline them." Too many people confuse love with 'nice', but they are very different.

Finally, one implication of this command which comes into sharp conflict with our culture today is that we should always promote life rather than death. There are, tragically, aspects of our society where taking life is permitted or even encouraged – in particular, abortion[33] and euthanasia[34]. To obey this command means that we should be prepared to stand against these things. That doesn't mean we need to become political activists – although God might call some of us to be –

---

[33] During 2020, the last year for which statistics are available at the time of writing, there were the highest number of abortions on record – 209,917.
[34] Euthanasia (including assisted dying or assisted suicide) is currently illegal but has a high level of public support and the case is often made for it in parliament and the media.

but we should use the opportunities God gives to stand for life where we can.

#7: You shall not commit adultery

This is another command which appears at face value to be straightforward. "Don't sleep with someone you're not married to" – job done. Or is it?

The New Testament speaks about "sexual immorality", which is a translation of the word *porneia* (where the word 'pornography' is derived from). Sexual immorality encompasses more than adultery – it includes things like prostitution (1 Corinthians 6:15-16), promiscuity (Galatians 5:19-21), and homosexuality (Romans 1:18-32). This command is not simply teaching about one aspect of sexual sin but includes every aspect of how we use our bodies sexually.

But it's not just sinful *actions* that are the problem. Let's think about what Jesus teaches in the Sermon on the Mount:

> You have heard that it was said, "You shall not commit adultery." But I tell you that anyone who looks at a woman lustfully has already committed adultery with her in his heart.
> *Matthew 5:27-28*

Jesus says here that the real sin is not adultery, but lust. Lust is a misuse of the desires that God has given us – in this instance, sexual desire. This is an especially important message to hear in our culture today, where lust is so pervasive and encouraged at virtually every point. Advertising, music videos, films and TV – it is normal for all of them to contain highly sexualised scenes and imagery. Not to mention the enormous problem of pornography. If you haven't seen the statistics, they are truly mind-boggling:

Today, porn sites receive more website traffic in the U.S. than Twitter, Instagram, Netflix, Pinterest, and LinkedIn combined.

Pornhub, one of the leading porn sites in the world, claimed that in 2019 they had 42 billion visitors with 39 billion searches performed. That's 115 million a day – almost 5 million an hour, and almost 80,000 a minute – and that's just one site. To put that in perspective, in the time it takes you to read this article, that one porn site will have recorded more than 200,000 visits, according to their own estimates. As for 2019 uploads to the site, PornHub estimates 12,500 gigabytes per minute – enough to fill the memories of every smart phone in the world.[35]

We live in an age which is sexualised like never before. We are bombarded with the message that the only thing which can fulfil our deepest desires is pornography. We are told that there is nothing bad about sexual desire – that whatever we want, we should be able to have. We're told that if you're not as fulfilled as could be, then perhaps you need to find a new partner. Is it any wonder that so many people are dissatisfied sexually? All this is deeply troubling to those who want to keep God's commands!

However, I believe that the church's response to the sexualisation of society has not always been very helpful or productive. The church has tended to double down on the 'thou shalt not' message: "don't do that, don't do that, *definitely* don't do that"! It is clear to see now, sixty years on from the sexual revolution, this is not a message which has had much of an impact. Even more tragically, the church is looking increasingly like the world.

---

[35] See online: https://fightthenewdrug.org/why-todays-internet-porn-is-unlike-anything-the-world-has-ever-seen/

This is where, once again, it's so important to see love behind the commands. There are several significant ways that Christians misunderstand this command.

Firstly, I have noticed that Christians often think obeying this command is equal to "get married" and "don't sleep with anyone else". However, I have seen too many Christian couples who are married and yet do not have a loving relationship, or who fantasise about being married to other people. People seem to think, "Well, of course I love my husband / wife, I'm married to them!" But this takes us back to Pharisaism. God gave us marriage in the law as a safeguard to protect against the worst aspects of human nature (i.e., unrestrained sexual desire). It acts as a kind of safety net, but *it is not the same as a loving relationship*. God never condones a loveless relationship or loveless sex.

I'm going to stick my neck out here and say that an unmarried couple who have a lifelong relationship of love are obeying this command, whereas a married couple who do not have a loving relationship are disobeying it. What matters to God is not a marriage certificate, but the presence (or absence) of love. Let me put it bluntly: **if you are married and yet do not love your husband or wife, you are not obeying this command.** Lest I be misunderstood, I am not advocating 'living together' instead of getting married in the way that many people do today. I am saying we need *more* love and commitment than a marriage certificate.

What does it mean to love your spouse? Many things! We should pray for them regularly, that God would help them and enable them to flourish. We should pray that God would help us to overcome our own inadequacies and grow in love. Marriage is a relationship of deep love and intimacy – why do we think we should be able to do it naturally, without God's help?

110

If we need God's help to love *in general,* how much more do you think we need God's help in our most intimate, loving relationship? This is where I believe a lot of Christian couples go wrong: they assume – with the world – that 'love' is something that just happens. But Christians should understand that is not true. As "love comes from God" (1 John 4:7), it is he alone who can help us. There's a beautiful prayer in the Church of England marriage service which recognises this truth:

> God of wonder and of joy:
> grace comes from you,
> and you alone are the source of life and love.
> Without you, we cannot please you;
> without your love, our deeds are worth nothing.
> Send your Holy Spirit,
> and pour into our hearts
>   that most excellent gift of love,
> that we may worship you now
> with thankful hearts
> and serve you always with willing minds;
> through Jesus Christ our Lord.

Christians should be known as those who have the most loving relationships, because we know the God who is love. As John puts it, "Whoever lives in love lives in God, and God in them" (1 John 4:16). If this is not the case even in our closest relationships, it should lead to genuine soul searching and heartfelt repentance.

Secondly, we need to realise that the solution to the problem of lust is not more rules. As we saw in Chapter Two, the Pharisees couldn't defeat sin by creating more rules: they didn't touch the heart of the issue. Unfortunately, we in the church have fallen into the bad habit of dealing with sexual temptation by setting more and more rules.

Let me give a few examples. Billy Graham would never eat a meal or otherwise spend time alone with a woman who was not his wife.[36] This may seem a noble way of wanting to avoid sexual temptation, but it has knock-on effects. An acquaintance of mine – a disabled man who is reliant upon others for transport – told me that he was unable to get a lift to church with a single woman because the church had a blanket policy of not allowing men and women to be alone together.

More recently, Aaron Renn has written about his personal rule of *never* having a one-on-one friendship with a woman:

> I will be super direct: other than actual sin, nothing else in my life has done me more harm than being friends with women. Nothing else even comes close. So I established a rigorous policy against it.[37]

If I may be super direct in response: establishing a rule like this to guard against sin is Pharisaism, pure and simple. As we saw earlier in the book, we do not combat sin by establishing more and more rules around the sin. That may prevent the symptoms (physical adultery) but will never deal with the root cause. **If we manage to avoid actual physical adultery but are still consumed by lust, we are not obeying God.**

As we saw in Chapter Five, the Biblical way to protect against lust is asking God to fill your heart with love. If you find yourself thinking lustful thoughts, especially if they are inspired by a particular person, ask God to replace those lustful thoughts with loving ones. Think about

---

[36] This is known as the Billy Graham Rule – it came to prominence in 2017 when it hit the news that US Vice President Mike Pence held to it.
[37] See online: https://aaronrenn.substack.com/p/newsletter-25-what-do-we-do-about

how you could *love* instead. You might be surprised to find that they really need your friendship.

My experience over the last few years is that many people are struggling with loneliness. I think an issue we are not talking enough about is that few people have healthy relationships with the opposite sex. There are many causes including family breakdown and the pervasive nature of pornography. Many men seem to find it difficult to even have a conversation with women. The sexual revolution has left a trail of devastation in its wake. The only thing that will bring healing is love, and that is only possible through the Holy Spirit – *not more rules*.

I have been pleasantly surprised to discover that there is a whole world waiting for those who trust in the power of the Spirit to transform us rather than relying on rules to keep us pure. I have enjoyed many more healthy relationships with the opposite sex than I would have been able to a few years ago. I ask God to help me love and be attentive to the needs of others. He answers those prayers: I do not constantly feel like I am living in 'dangerous' territory; rather, I feel that God is guiding me all the way and I can entrust myself to him.

I appreciate that I have spoken at length about this command, but I believe it is perhaps the most important of the "love your neighbour" commands to listen to in our sexualised world. It is also the command that I think many Christians struggle most with. Sex is held up as an idol by our secular culture. But, rather than giving in to secular gods, Christians have a huge opportunity to demonstrate that sex is not god, and that God can enable us to do that which the world cannot do. It is by trusting in the power of God, through the Holy Spirit, that we overcome our lusts and love one another in every way.

#8: You shall not steal

This is another command which, on the surface, appears to be straightforward. Everyone would agree that taking something without the owner's consent is theft and is therefore wrong. It is even against the law. Most of us are not thieves and robbers. So, is this another command that we can skip over, safe in the knowledge that it doesn't apply to us?

Once again, we need to think more deeply. For one thing, it is possible to take from someone else without taking a material possession. For example, have you ever taken the credit for something which rightly belonged to someone else? Or have you ever been happy to accept an opportunity which should have gone to someone else?

When we include God as someone we can steal from, it becomes even more clear. God gives us everything that we have (James 1:17); he also bought us at a price (1 Corinthians 6:20). Because we belong to him, we do not have liberty to use our bodies, gifts, money and possessions however we want to. We should use them according to his will. Therefore, when we do not use them rightly, *it is theft*. We are taking away what rightly belongs to him.

This command also has implications for the way that we should love others. Let's return to the Heidelberg Catechism:

> I must promote my neighbour's good
>   wherever I can and may,
> deal with him
>   as I would like others to deal with me,
> and work faithfully

so that I may be able to give
to those in need.[38]

Obeying this command means more than to avoid harming our neighbour, but actively promoting their good instead. When it comes to their possessions, this might mean defending them. For example, if you see your neighbour's house being burgled, don't sit there and do nothing – call the police!

The most important word when it comes to our material things is *generosity*. The command says we should not take away from our neighbour what belongs to them. As the Catechism points out, we should go further and in fact work so that we may have something that we can give. This is taken from the Bible:

> Anyone who has been stealing must steal no longer, but must work, doing something useful with their own hands, that they may have something to share with those in need.
> *Ephesians 4:28*

Our attitudes should be transformed. Rather than envying other people's things and taking them for ourselves, we should sit lightly to the things that we have and use them for the good of others. A selfish attitude is transformed into a loving and generous attitude.

#9: Do not bear false witness

When I was a child, this command was taught to me as 'do not lie'. That is a good simplification for a child, but the truth is rather more complicated. The exact words of the command are, "you shall not give false testimony against your neighbour". In other words, this is the

---

[38] See online: http://www.heidelberg-catechism.com/en/lords-days/42.html

language of the courtroom rather than everyday life. We are commanded not to bring a false charge or slander our neighbour publicly.

You could say, if the previous commands were to prevent us from harming others with actions, this command is to prevent us from harming them with *words*. We are to use words to love others and build them up, rather than to tear down and destroy. This happens when we speak the truth to one another:

> Instead, speaking the truth in love, we will grow to become in
> every respect the mature body of him who is the head, that is,
> Christ.
> *Ephesians 4:15*

"Speaking the truth in love" – this is a beautiful, succinct phrase of what we should be like. Rather than using our words to tear down and wound our neighbour, we should use our words to speak truthfully – especially God's Word – and so build up our neighbour.

The reason this is so important is because lies are from Satan. Jesus said:

> You belong to your father, the devil, and you want to carry out
> your father's desires. He was a murderer from the beginning, not
> holding to the truth, for there is no truth in him. When he lies, he
> speaks his native language, for he is a liar and the father of lies.
> *John 8:44*

Lies come from Satan, whereas the truth comes from God. In fact, lying is anathema to God – the Bible says God "does not lie" (Titus 1:2). If we wish to be like our heavenly Father, we should be devoted to the truth in every respect.

It's important to say that a devotion to the truth doesn't mean a life free of conflict. In fact, it's rather the opposite! Sadly, the truth can put us at odds with other people. And sometimes, the truth can hurt: as the Proverb says, "Wounds from a friend can be trusted, but an enemy multiplies kisses" (Proverbs 27:6). Sometimes we need to speak the truth to someone, truth which we know is going to hurt them. So, speaking the truth isn't saying "let's all be nice to everyone and never offend them" – but rather, love should motivate us always to speak what is right and true *even if it costs us.*

What are the wider implications of "speaking the truth in love"? Let's turn back to the words of the Heidelberg Catechism:

> I must not give false testimony against anyone,
>> twist no one's words,
>> not gossip or slander,
>> nor condemn or join in condemning anyone
>> rashly and unheard.
> Rather, I must avoid all lying and deceit
>> as the devil's own works,
>> under penalty of God's heavy wrath.
> In court and everywhere else,
> I must love the truth,
>> speak and confess it honestly,
>> and do what I can
>> to defend and promote
>> my neighbour's honour and reputation.[39]

These words, written centuries ago, have an astonishing significance to the twenty-first century. I think these words should be in the terms and

---

[39] See online: http://www.heidelberg-catechism.com/en/lords-days/43.html

conditions for anyone using social media. It's very easy to join in condemning someone "rashly and unheard" online. It's also very easy to not promote our neighbour's honour and reputation online. We must seek always to speak and defend the truth where we can, as an act of love.

#10: Do not covet

In this final command, we are introduced to a word we don't use very much these days – "covet":

> You shall not covet your neighbour's house. You shall not covet your neighbour's wife, or his male or female servant, his ox or donkey, or anything that belongs to your neighbour.
> *Exodus 20:17*

Coveting basically means wanting something we don't have. But it's more than wanting as in, "I want a drink of water", but *wanting* to the point that it might lead to a wrong action. For example, if you covet your neighbour's wife, you might commit adultery with her. If you covet your neighbour's property, you might steal it from him. In this way, coveting is intimately linked with the previous commandments.

In some ways, this command could have been designed for the twenty-first century: we are bombarded with advertising messages all the time which are designed to make us dissatisfied with the things we have. But the problem is more than simple desire. It's not wrong to want things – there are all sorts of things we need and want. The problem is wanting the wrong things, or perhaps wanting the right things but in the wrong way. This gets to the root of the problem with us as human beings – sin starts with our desires. James says:

> When tempted, no one should say, 'God is tempting me.' For God cannot be tempted by evil, nor does he tempt anyone; but each person is tempted when they are dragged away by their own evil desire and enticed. Then, after desire has conceived, it gives birth to sin; and sin, when it is full-grown, gives birth to death.
> *James 1:13-15*

As we've seen all the way through this book, sinful actions start with sinful desires. When we desire the wrong things, or when we desire the right things but in the wrong ways, we sin. We don't even have to get to the action for it to be sin – it's enough simply to have the desire.

This is why Paul says:

> Put to death, therefore, whatever belongs to your earthly nature: sexual immorality, impurity, lust, evil desires and greed, which is idolatry.
> *Colossians 3:5*

The word "greed" could also be translated "covetousness" – it's a similar concept. Paul is saying that coveting is idolatry. It is idolatrous because it seeks to fulfil desires in a sinful way rather than a godly way. We should take all our desires to the Lord and trust him to give us the things that we need. He is a good Father and knows how to give good gifts to those who ask him (Matthew 7:11). He knows what we need before we ask (Matthew 6:8). God wants us to take our desires to him, rather than ignoring them and becoming resentful or trying to fulfil them without him.

I am convinced that the cause of all sin ultimately is the belief that God is not good and will not give us the things that we need or want. This was the problem Adam and Eve had in the Garden of Eden: the serpent convinced them that God was not good and did not have their best interests at heart. They tried to get what was good for themselves apart from God, rather than allowing God to determine what was good for them. They believed that God was withholding something good from them, rather than being the generous giver of all good gifts. You could say the problem was covetousness.

What this command is saying, then, is that we should pour out our heart's desires before the Lord and trust him to fulfil them, rather than seeking to hold onto them ourselves. We should have the same attitude of David:

> Praise the Lord, my soul;
>   all my inmost being, praise his holy name.
> Praise the Lord, my soul,
>   and forget not all his benefits –
> who forgives all your sins
>   and heals all your diseases,
> who redeems your life from the pit
>   and crowns you with love and compassion,
> who satisfies your desires with good things
>   so that your youth is renewed like the eagle's.
> *Psalm 103:1-5*

As we come to truly know the Lord as a good and generous Father, we will be able to praise him for all his blessings. A living relationship with the Lord is the antidote to coveting – which brings us back to the first commandments. As we enjoy a relationship with the living God, as we love him and love others, and as we bring our hearts to him, he will satisfy us with his goodness. This command, in a sense, ties all the previous commands together into one package.

Summary

I appreciate this has been a long chapter. I hope there has been plenty of food for thought here, but I also know it's a lot to take in. In case it seems overwhelming, I thought it might be helpful to zoom out and take a bird's eye view.

- The first three commands are about our relationship with God: we should put him first, worship him truly, and worship him authentically with our lives.
- The fourth command is a transition, about how we should show our love for God and others in the way that we use our time.
- The fifth command is how we can show love for others by honouring our families and respecting appropriate authority.
- The sixth to ninth commands show that we love and honour others:
  - With our bodies
  - With our sexuality
  - With possessions and material things
  - With our words
- The tenth commandment brings us back to the beginning and says we should not covet – which would lead us to do wrong – but instead bring our desires to the Lord.

The most important thing to remember, once again, is that **obedience does not come from within ourselves**. Our obedience comes as we repent of our sins and turn to Christ to forgive us. He alone cleanses us of our sin and gives us power, through the Holy Spirit, to bear the fruit of love in our lives.

If you read this section on the Ten Commandments and think, "I need to try harder" – you've got it wrong! I have included this chapter to help us see where we fall short and where we need to repent. This is not about needing to work harder so that God will accept us! Remember that Christ Jesus is our righteousness. Our obedience should come from a heart of love, knowing that God *has* forgiven us. We do not need to fear, uncertain if we've done enough for God to accept us. We simply need to trust and walk with the One who loves us every day. This is the way that we grow in obedience.

I also need to emphasize that this chapter is not supposed to be the last word on the commandments. We need to spend time meditating on God's law, in the power of the Holy Spirit, to help us know the areas in our lives that God wants to work on. I hope this chapter has been helpful in meditating on the law, but it is not a substitute for thinking it through (and, indeed, praying it through) yourself.

Chapter Seven: Church – a community of love

As we come to the close of this book, I want to paint two contrasting pictures of what life could be like. I hope this will help us to comprehend the difference that grace should make in our lives and our communities.

The first picture is of what life would be like if we simply tried to keep the rules as best we could.

A rules-based approach, as the Pharisees adopted, is designed to avoid doing anything harmful to other people. We don't want to murder them, steal from them, commit adultery with them, and so on. We want to avoid all wrongdoing. However, we can be so keen to avoid wrongdoing that we end up avoiding other people completely.

If we take the analogy I used in the first chapter about friendship between men and women, it leads to the kind of attitude which says: "to avoid lust, I will *always* avoid being alone with the opposite sex". Even if that means you can't do something basic such as give lifts to church, let alone befriend someone who might be desperately lonely and in need. When we fear what might happen, we draw back from others and end up becoming less human.

This is uncomfortably close to C.S. Lewis' vision of hell from his book *The Great Divorce*. In the book, Lewis imagines hell as a vast yet sparsely populated city where people keep moving away from each other. They cannot bear to be close to one another, and so choose isolation instead of community. This is what a world without love would look like – and it's a world which Pharisaism starts to resemble.

This is not God's way. We know this ultimately because of Jesus Christ. John says:

> Dear friends, let us love one another, for love comes from God. Everyone who loves has been born of God and knows God. Whoever does not love does not know God, because God is love. This is how God showed his love among us: He sent his one and only Son into the world that we might live through him. This is love: not that we loved God, but that he loved us and sent his Son as an atoning sacrifice for our sins. Dear friends, since God so loved us, we also ought to love one another. No one has ever seen God; but if we love one another, God lives in us and his love is made complete in us.
> *1 John 4:7-12*

"Whoever does not love does not know God". These are hard words, but necessary for us to hear. What is love? That God sent his son as an atoning sacrifice for our sins. God did not stay at a distance to avoid hurting us. He sent his son into the middle of our messy world, so that we might be redeemed. He sent his son so that we might be able to love one another. In fact, love is *the* distinguishing mark of what it means to truly know God. As Jesus said: "By this everyone will know that you are my disciples, if you love one another" (John 13:35).

Love is not an optional extra for the Christian life. It's something which God gives, through Jesus Christ, in the power of the Holy Spirit. It should fill us and our communities, it should set us apart from the world. Too often the church has been filled instead with a spirit of fear – a spirit of keeping our distance from our brothers and sisters. This is not true Christian community.

By contrast, the second picture I want to paint is of a truly loving, Christian, community. A place where each person can confess their sins to the Lord and find a new strength to love. A place where nobody feels left out, where everyone is able to flourish in holiness and righteousness. A place where we can support one another in our struggles and battles, building authentic and meaningful relationships, with the Lord at the centre. A place which feels more like our family than our biological family. Somewhere we can praise God together and share all his good gifts with one another.

I believe this kind of community is not a pipe dream – it is the kind of community that God calls us to. God does not call us to be a team of individuals, he calls us to be his new holy people. As Peter says:

> But you are a chosen people, a royal priesthood, a holy
> nation, God's special possession, that you may declare the
> praises of him who called you out of darkness into his
> wonderful light. Once you were not a people, but now you are
> the people of God; once you had not received mercy, but now
> you have received mercy.
> *1 Peter 2:9-10*

We are no longer isolated individuals, only chasing our own dreams and desires. God has called us to play a full part in his church, to put each other first, to love one another. In the words of Keith & Kristyn Getty:

> Beneath the cross of Jesus,
> His family is my own.

Once strangers chasing selfish dreams;
Now, one through grace alone.
How could I now dishonour
The ones that You have loved?
Beneath the cross of Jesus,
See the children called by God.

The cross takes us as individuals who seek our own fulfilment, our own desires, our own dreams, and transforms us into those who want to love and build up God's people around us. We cannot obey God's commands in isolation: they can only be obeyed in community. As we repent of our sinfulness and come to God, we receive the help of the Holy Spirit to make us more loving and outward focussed.

As God's chosen people, those who belong to the Lord Jesus, let's resolve to walk together in love. Let's set aside fear and instead seek the help of the Holy Spirit to do that which we cannot do by nature. Let's show the world what it truly means to "love one another deeply, from the heart" (1 Peter 1:22), as God has showed his love to us in Jesus Christ.

About the Author

Phill originally trained in Computer Science and worked as a software developer for several years before going back to theological college and training for ordination. He was ordained in the Church of England in 2014. He currently spends part of his time serving a church on the Essex coast and the rest running a Christian ministry called Understand the Bible.

Understand the Bible

Understand the Bible began a few years ago when Phill started creating YouTube videos to give to people who'd done an outreach course at church. In 2019 he had the opportunity to dedicate some time to the project and Understand the Bible was born. Since then, he has completed courses on "What is Christianity?", the Ten Commandments, the Lord's Prayer, and the Apostle's Creed. The objective is to help people from every stage establish deep roots in the Christian faith.

Find it online: <u>understandthebible.uk</u>

Printed in Great Britain
by Amazon

20340272R00078